W9-ATL-547

MYTH
AND
RELIGION

THE EDITED TRANSCRIPTS

Charles E. Tuttle Co., Inc.
Boston ✦ Rutland, Vermont ✦ Tokyo

Published in the United States in 1996 by
Charles E. Tuttle Company, Inc. of Rutland, Vermont & Tokyo, Japan,
with editorial offices at 153 Milk Street, Boston, Massachusetts 02109.

Library of Congress Catalog Card number 96–60087
ISBN 0–8048–3055–X

Photo courtesy of Alan Watts Electronic Educational Programs

First Edition

00 99 98 97 96   1 3 5 7 9 10 8 6 4 2

Printed in the United States of America

MYTH
AND
RELIGION

THE EDITED TRANSCRIPTS

Alan Watts

ALAN WATTS
at a seminar aboard the SS *Vallejo,* 1966

Western civilization is in a state of chaos. It has lost effective knowledge of man's true nature and destiny. Neither philosophy nor religion as they are known today do much to give man the consciousness that the deepest center or "ground" of his being is to be found in that eternal reality which is in the West called God.

—Alan Watts, 1951

CONTENTS

During his last television appearance in 1973 Alan Watts was asked what it was he found lacking in modern Christianity that led him toward Far Eastern philosophies, and he replied that it was an experiential basis. Simply put, the knowledge of transcendental or mystical experience has been lost in the mythology of modern Western religions, and with it has disappeared the original source of spiritual authority.

In the West ultimate authority is based on "the word of God" as it has been handed down to us as part of a mythology in which humans are the creations of a mighty father image symbolic of the powers of heaven. In contrast, most original tribal religions worship the Earth powers as the source of creation. Typically Western myths are intellectually abstract. However, in the Far East, doctrine is regarded as secondary to the student's direct experience of enlightenment. Zen masters are legendary in their insistence on the "original mind," and the famous "koan method" of instruction is dedicated exclusively to achieving liberation. As Huston Smith wrote in his introduction to *The Zen Eye*, a collection of talks by Sokei-an Sasaki,

> *It is the distinguishing genius of Zen Buddhism*
> *(and its Chinese antecedent, Ch'an) to refuse to*
> *dislodge earth from heaven. That emphasis is*
> *(in its degree) unique within the historical reli-*
> *gions, but it is the way tribal, pre-writing peo-*
> *ples see things regularly. Considered in this*
> *light, Ch'an and Zen are rivulets that perpetu-*
> *ate, in history, an early talent.*

In this volume of his edited transcripts, Alan Watts brings the question of spiritual authority sharply into focus. Continuing in the tradition of mystics and sages who point to a direct connection between man and God, he identifies the individual as the true source of religion.

In this light he discusses the historical Jesus and examines the nature of the "religion about Jesus" as it has evolved since biblical times. Watts goes on to examine the subtle meaning of the "God is dead" theology, which emerged out of a dissatisfaction with a religion "about Jesus" that failed to offer a mystical experience. Here he identifies a striking similarity between the most hopeful expressions of the "God is dead" concept and the essential teaching of Buddhism. Recalling the teacher who told his students, "If you meet Buddha on the road,

kill him," he challenges Christian practitioners to abandon intellectual idolatry—in which dogma is favored
over a direct, personal experience of the transcendental—and suggests, as one exercise for bringing about the
abandonment of this idolatry, that Christians consider
burning the Bible every Easter as an affirmation of true
faith.

In contrast to this suggested ritual, Watts describes
the actual ritual of his initiation into the Church of
England. As the reader will see, this ceremony lacked the
qualities that distinguish the passage of a young man
into adulthood that are common to cultures in which
personal mystical experience is respected. Given this, one
wonders whether the state of chaos in which modern
civilization finds itself might not be the result of the failure of our culture to encourage the transition through
adolescence into adulthood, with the result that our culture is now one in which personal development is rou-
tinely arrested in early adolescence. We see this in our
worship of youth, and as Alan Watts points out, attachment to the body formed in youth is a denial of the
transformative power of life.

This volume will guide the reader toward an
encounter with the transcendental source of true religion
and, through it, away from the chaos of our present
predicament.

—Mark Watts,
San Anselmo, California

MYTH
AND
RELIGION

THE EDITED TRANSCRIPTS

I take the liberty of beginning by saying something about myself and my role in talking about philosophical matters, because I want to make it perfectly clear that I am not a guru. In other words, I talk about what we call "these things" that comprise a multitude of interests concerning Oriental philosophy, psychotherapy, religion, and mysticism because I am interested in them and because I enjoy talking about them, and that explains me. In saying that I am not a guru, that means I am not trying to help you or improve you. I accept you as you are. I am not out to save the world. Of course, when a stream, a bubbling spring, flows out from the mountains, it is doing its thing. And if a thirsty traveler helps himself, that is fine. When a bird sings, it does not sing for the advancement of music. But if somebody stops to listen, and is delighted, that is fine. And I talk in the same spirit.

I am not trying to create disciples. I work on the principle of a physician rather than a clergyman. A physician is always trying to get rid of his patients and send them away healthy to stand on their own feet. A clergyman is trying to get them as members of a religious organization, so that they will continue to pay the clergy, pay off the mortgage on an expensive building, and generally belong to the church, boost its membership, and thereby prove by sheer weight of numbers the veracity of its tenants. My objective is really to get rid of you so that you won't need me or any other teacher. I am afraid some of my colleagues would not approve of that attitude because it is widely said that in order to advance in the spiritual life, whatever that is, it is essential that you have a guru, and that you accord to that guru perfect obedience.

I am often asked the question, "Is it really necessary to have a guru?" I can answer that only by saying, "It is necessary, if you think so." That is said in the same spirit as one might say that anybody who goes to a psychiatrist ought to have his head examined. There is more in that saying than meets the ear, because if you really are sincerely concerned with yourself, and are in such confusion that you feel you have to go to a psychiatrist to talk over your state, then of course you need to go. Likewise, if you are in need of someone to tell you how to practice meditation, or to attain a state of liberation, nirvana, *moksha,* or whatever it may be called, and if you feel that necessity very strongly, then you must do it because, as the poet William Blake said, "The fool who persists in his folly will become wise." However, I do want to ask you, What is the source of a guru's authority? He can tell you that he speaks from experience, that he has experienced states of consciousness that have made him profoundly blissful, understanding, compassionate, or whatever. You have his word for it and you may have the word of other people who likewise agree with him. But each one of them, and you in turn, agrees with him from out of your own opinion, and by your own judgment. So it is you who are the source of the teacher's authority. That is true whether he speaks as an individual or as the representative of a tradition or a church.

You may say that you take the Bible as your authority, or the Roman Catholic Church, and the Roman Catholic follower very often says that the individual mystical experience is not to be trusted, because of its tendency to be interpreted in a purely personal way; it is the substantial and objective traditions of the church that will guard against these excesses. However, those traditions are held to be substantial and objective only because followers of those traditions believe them to be so. They say they are so, and if you follow them, you are also saying they are. The question comes back to you. Why do you believe; why do you form this opinion; upon what basis does all this rest?

Almost everybody is looking for help, except, "When I was younger, so much younger than today, I never needed anybody's help in any way." But there is this feeling of a certain helplessness, of being alone and somewhat confused in an unpredictable, wayward, external world of happenings. This world of happenings includes an enormous amount of suffering and tragedy. We wonder why we are here, how we got here, and in short, what to do about the "problem of life," to which should be added the problem of death, because it seems to be certain that we are all going to die, and those we

3

love are going to die, and that death and dying may be a painful process. Is there any way in which we can become masters of this situation?

There are all sorts of ways of trying to escape from the human predicament, which is that of a lonely, isolated consciousness in the midst of an enormous non-self. We can try to beat the game on a material basis by becoming very wealthy or very powerful. We may resort to all kinds of technology to get rid of our sufferings: hunger, pain, sickness, and so forth. But it will be noticed that as we succeed in these enterprises, we are not satisfied. In other words, if you feel at this time that an increase in income would solve your problems, and you got that increase in income, this would give you a pleasant feeling for a few weeks. But then, as you well know if that has ever happened to you, the feeling wears off. You may stop worrying about paying your debts, and start worrying about whether you will get sick. There is always something to worry about. Even if you are very rich indeed, you will still have anxiety about sickness and death, and also anxieties about whether the Internal Revenue Service will take all your money away from you, or catch you for cheating on your taxes, or put you in prison for no good reason. There is always such worry.

You realize that the problem of life does not really consist in your external circumstances. You will worry, whatever your external circumstances will be. Rather, the problem consists in what you call your mind. Could you, by some method, control your mind so that you won't worry? How on earth would you do that? Some people tell you that the best answer is to think positive thoughts, to be peaceful, to breathe slowly and hum gently, and to get yourself into a peaceful state of mind by repeating affirmations such as "All is light," "All is

God," "All is good," or whatever. But unfortunately that doesn't always work, because you may still have a nagging suspicion in the back of your mind that you are simply hypnotizing yourself and whistling in the dark. This is what in German is called a *hintegedanka,* which is the thought—concealed way back behind your intellect—that has a gnawing persistence.

Perhaps you realize that this matter of controlling of the mind is no superficial undertaking, because although you may be able to smooth the ruffles of your consciousness, beneath that is a vast area of unconsciousness, which erupts as unpredictably as events in the external world. You may consider seriously the possibilities of psychoanalysis, of going down into those depths to see if oil can be put on those troubled waters. Perhaps then you will look into going to some guru against whose mirror you can reflect those aspects of yourself of which you are not directly aware.

As the process goes on, you may find there is something awkward about all this. This awkwardness can be expressed in many different ways. One is this: How on earth are you to get at yourself, to do something about yourself? This is a project not unlike trying to pierce the point of the pin with the point of the same pin.

In other words, if you feel that you need to make some sort of psychological or spiritual improvement, obviously you are the character who is going to have to bring this about. But if you are the one who needs to be improved, how are you going to accomplish the improvement? You are in the predicament of trying to lift yourself up off the floor by pulling at your own bootstraps, and you are likely to land with a bang on your fanny and end up lower down than you were in the first place.

This problem continually arises, and it has arisen historically in all the great religious traditions. We find it in Christianity, in Saint Augustine, who replied to the argument "God would not have given us a commandment to love him, and to love our neighbors, if we could obey it," by answering, "Yes, but the commandment was not given in order for it to be obeyed. God never expected that it would be obeyed, because we were incapable of loving anyone but ourselves." The commandment was therefore given to convince us of our sinfulness from which we could be rescued only by divine grace, by the infusion of our souls with a power beyond them. That was more or less the doctrine on which the church settled. Therefore the puzzle has always been how to get grace. Grace is apparently freely offered to all, but some people get it, and some don't. With some, the medicine takes, and with others it doesn't. Apparently you have the power to resist grace, but if you do, you also have the power to accept it. We would like therefore to know how to accept it, to be open.

This brings us back to exactly the same place we began. It is like saying "You must relax, damn you. Let go! Give in!" Of course I know I ought to give in; I know I ought to let go, abandon my will to the divine will. But as Saint Paul puts it so well, "The will is present with me, but how to do that which is good, I find not. For the good that I would do, I do not, and the evil that I would not do, that I do." In other words, we all come down to something in ourselves that is called the *yetzer ha-ra,* the wayward spirit that God is supposed to have put into the soul of Adam. In my translation, it is our element of "irreducible rascality." We are all basically scamps in one way or another. I know all sorts of people who are full of outward virtue, but it always turns out that they need money. Of course, when it comes to money, virtue flies out the window. We do have an element of rascality in ourselves; we know it very well. The question again is How can it be transformed? If the transformer is also the one who is afflicted, how can the afflicted be transformed? It is the old problem of who guards the guards, who polices the police, who governs the government? It is a vicious circle. There is a great deal of talk about our having two selves, a lower self or ego, and a higher self called the spirit or the atman. The duty of the atman seems to be to transform the wretched little ego. Sometimes it does, but many times it doesn't. So we might ask, "Why doesn't So-and-so's atman succeed in getting through? Is his ego too strong? If so, who will weaken it? Is his atman too weak, and if so, how can that be, for surely aren't all atmans the same?" Still, the puzzle remains.

Let us take a look at what we are trying to accomplish by this. We are trying to get better. We seek out those types of experiences that we call the positive, the good, the light, the living, and we wish to avoid the negative, the evil, the dark, and the dead. Unfortunately, we are equipped with a nervous system in which the neurons either fire or don't fire. Everything we are aware of is created out of an extremely complicated arrangement of yes and no. We can put colored television on tape so that it is all reduced to a matter of yes and no. And that, you will understand, is the philosophy of the Chinese Book of Changes, the *I Ching,* which represents all the situations of life in terms of combinations of yang, or the positive principle, and yin, the negative. Interestingly enough, the Latin translation of the *I Ching* was read by the philosopher Leibniz, and from this he invented binary arithmetic, in which all numbers can be represented by zero and one, which is the number system used by the digital computer that lies behind all our electronic ingenuity.

Our great extension of the nervous system is based on the same principle.

Can you see, then, what we are trying to do when we seek the positive and avoid the negative? We are trying to have yang without yin. We are trying to arrange a life game in which there is winning without losing. How can you arrange such a state of affairs? If we are all equally happy, it is impossible to know that we are happy, because a certain flatness will come over everything. If we lifted up all valleys, and lowered all mountains, we should have the sort of destruction of the ecology that they are achieving with bulldozers in the Hollywood Hills, in ghastly fulfillment of the biblical prophecy that every valley should be exalted and every mountain laid low, and the rough places made even. But Isaiah also said something that Christians, at least, do not often quote, which is, "I am the Lord, and there is none else. I form the light and create the darkness. I make peace and I create evil. I, the Lord, do all these things." In spite of this, everybody is busy trying to be good, not realizing that we would not recognize saints unless there were sinners, or sages unless there were fools. There is no way out of that dilemma.

Buddhism represents existence in terms of a wheel, called the *pavarachakra,* the wheel of becoming, of birth and death. On the top of that wheel are *devas* who we could call angels. At the bottom of the wheel there are *naraka,* or tormented people in purgatory. You go round and round, now this way, now that. It is really like a squirrel cage, where you are running and running to get to the top, and you have to run faster and faster just to stay where you are. That is why there is always the sense that the more you succeed in any scale of either worldly or spiritual progress, the more you are still in the same place. Perhaps there is something ambitious, proud, and wrong in aspiring to be enlightened or compassionate. Perhaps there is a great dose of spiritual pride in thinking that I, by my efforts, could make myself into a buddha or a saint. Therefore, perhaps the thing to do is to try to eliminate all desire, not only the desire for worldly success, but also for spiritual success. The Buddha proposed that desire was the root of suffering, and therefore suggested to his disciples that if they eliminated desire or clinging, they might cease from suffering. But you must realize that the teachings of the Buddha are not doctrines in the sense that the Jews and the Christians and the Moslems have doctrines. They are proposals. They are the opening steps in a dialogue. If you go away and try to cease desiring, you will very quickly discover that you are desiring not to desire. So you very rapidly come to a situation where you discover that with regard to your own transformation, everything you try fails to work. Some sort of temporary success may make you feel better, but again and again you will still come back to the same old gnawing problem. That is why people interested in spiritual things tend to move from one sect to another, from one teacher to another, always hoping that they will meet the one who has the answer for them.

Indeed, many teachers say, "There is nothing you can do." Then you have to practice nondoing, what the Taoists call *wu wei*, nonstriving. Of course, you will find that it is extraordinarily difficult not to strive. It is like trying not to think of a green elephant; immediately you think of one. You come to the dismal conclusion that you can neither achieve liberation from the alternation of opposites by striving, nor can you achieve it by not striving. It is like trying to be unselfconscious through an act of will, or to be genuine, or to love. It puts you in a double bind. When we say of a person that he has trained himself to be deliberately unselfconscious and that he has very disciplined spontaneity, we are looking for somebody whose spontaneity is genuine, so that the scaffolding does not show. We believe that there are such people. Like children, they do not know how interesting they are, but when they find out, they become brats.

Imagine for a moment that it is your privilege to have a brief interview with God, in the course of which you are allowed to ask one question. What would you ask? You would have to think this over very carefully, because this golden opportunity would come to you only once, and you would have to be most careful not to ask a silly question. You might try God out with a Zen Buddhist koan such as "Beyond the positive and the negative, what is reality?" The Lord would turn to you and say, "My dear child, your question has no meaning." And you would not have the opportunity to think up a meaningful response.

Perhaps you should have asked, "What question should I ask?" And the Lord would say to you, "Why do you want to have a question?" You want one because you would feel that something was wrong if you didn't have one. But you have got a question: the insoluble problem of trying to win without losing, and as long as you have that problem you will be kept busy, until you see that it is meaningless because it cannot be solved. However, there are all sorts of ways of thinking about that problem in ways so as to prevent yourself from seeing that it is meaningless.

The better gurus are very clever at bringing these ways out. If you are invited to practice intense concentration, after a while you may find yourself thinking about concentrating, and therefore see that your concentration is somewhat divided. The guru may ask, "Why are you concentrating? What is your motivation for this activity?" And you may find out that the answer is your irreducible rascality. However, the teacher, once he has seen that you have mastered that lesson, has something still more ingenuous to teach. He says, "You have made progress. Finding out that you cannot concentrate has begun to prick the illusion of your ego, but you have only got your foot in the door. Beyond this are many higher learnings, and you must redouble your efforts." And so you apply yourself all the more, again and again, to all sorts of tricks that these old gentlemen can come up with. You keep at it as long as he can make you fall for it, but in the end, you see that it was all tricks.

The great Zen master Rinzai said, "After all, there was nothing much in Obaku's Buddhism." He went on to explain to his students that the art of Zen, or teaching Zen, is like deceiving a child with an empty fist. You know how you intrigue a child by pretending you have something very precious in your fist. You can play this game for an hour, provoking the child to ever greater enthusiasm to find out what you have. At the end, the revelation is that nothing was there. Many people say in the course of their Zen training, "I realize there was nothing to realize. It was all there from the beginning." Standing opposite this realization—that you cannot do anything about your desires, and equally that you cannot do nothing about them—is the awakening that this realization is true because there is no you separate from you. In other words, when you try to control your thoughts, or feelings, there is no difference between the thoughts and the controller. What you call the thinker is simply your thought of yourself. The thinker is a thought among thoughts, and the feeler is a feeling among feelings, but trying to control thoughts with thoughts is like trying to bite your own teeth.

The other side of the picture is that when you do discover that the project of controlling yourself was unnecessary, it will be because you were yourself a Buddha from the very beginning. That is what the Upanishads mean when they say quite simply *Tat tvam asi*—"You are it"—you, as you are. How can you conceive that? Suppose you let your imagination go, and really think through what you would like to have happen. Imagine the most gorgeous state of bliss that you can conceive, where there are no worries, no anxieties, and no haunting future with unpleasant consequences. You are in control of the whole works, and you are sitting on your lotus, perfectly content. I ask you seriously, are you quite sure that is really what you want? Imagine the situation. You have everything you want. You are in the highest possible spiritual state that you can conceive, and yet you have not really surrendered yourself, because you know everything.

The feeling of self depends on there being, at the same time, a contrasting feeling of other. The self has a sensation of being in control of life to some extent through voluntary action. The will seems to have a certain freedom, and yet on the other hand, there are limits. It seems that in the end, life sweeps us away. We are overwhelmed by the involuntary, yet the voluntary keeps popping up. New voluntaries come into the world with every baby. So you could not have the experience you call "being a voluntarily acting self" without the contrast of the involuntary happening. Would you want to be without the involuntary happening? If you could get rid of that, you wouldn't have the experience of the voluntary self. To turn it the other way around, would you like to have the experience of no voluntary self, where everything just happens? You may say, "I'm not sure about that, because then I would feel that I was just walking on air, floating along, with no further responsibilities."

Of course, we do get that feeling sometimes. If you take the ideas of determinism and fatalism to their final conclusion, you do have that sense of freedom from all responsibilities, from worry and care. However, it wears off, and it seems to be impossible to follow out that philosophy consistently, especially if you have children. Somehow society begins to push you to be responsible, just as it pushes children to be responsible, and this nagging duality keeps returning. I cannot realize the irresponsible condition of involuntary life unless I have the contrast of the possibility of the voluntary, and vice versa.

These two aspects of our experience—which we can call the voluntary and the involuntary, the knower and the known, the subject and the object, the self and the other—although appearing to be two, are indeed one. You cannot have one without the other. Whenever it seems that you do, you should know at once that there is a conspiracy, that when two things seem as different as different can be, they are actually, for that very reason, the same. You can detect this even within those actions that you call voluntary. In the voluntary movement of the muscles or of the mind there are processes that are not voluntary. You do not will your blood to circulate, you do not control by intention the synapses in your nervous system, and yet you would be incapable of any voluntary action unless those involuntary processes were going on. So, therefore, these differences go together.

You begin to realize something that is rather difficult to describe: that what you call your experience is a do-happening. We do not have good words for this. We have some words that convey this sense, like the word *cleave,* which means "to stick together" or "to hold together" and also "to split." So I would like to propose we find some word for a do-happening, because everything is a do-happening.

When Buddhists talk about karma, they mean action, and when something happens to you, be it good or bad, they say it is your karma. That means quite simply, "It is your doing." Now, you may say, "I did not mean to do that." One school of thought will explain events by saying, "You did something in a former life, or at a former time, that is now having this consequence." However, that is a very superficial understanding of karma. You do not need to believe in reincarnation to understand karma. Karma is simply not letting your left hand know what your right hand is doing. With one aspect you are doing what you call the environment, and with the other aspect you are doing what you call the organism, this living body. Since you cannot possibly conceive of the existence of a living body with no environment, there is the clue that the two are basically one. As with the two poles of a magnet, north is quite different from south, and yet they are both part of one magnet.

In precisely the same way, you are both what you do and what happens to you. You have a little game in which you play that you are not responsible for what happens to you, you are only responsible for what you do. This illusion allows you to compete with the two sides of yourself. It is like getting two knitting pins, one in each hand, and having a fencing match with yourself. If you sincerely try to stick one hand with the other, the first hand must really try to stick the other, just to defend itself. You will come to a sort of standstill, unless you decide that your right hand is the one that is going to win, and then you have broken the rules of the game, which is what we do all the time.

Both the Hindus and the Buddhists call this rule-breaking *avidya*, "ignorance," which really means *ignore*ance. Basically it comes down to the fact that you are responsible for everything. The guru's authority comes from you. The place in life where you are is where you have put yourself. Just as on the surface of the sphere every point may be regarded as the center of the surface, so every place may be regarded as the true place. Everyone is in their true place. In whatever language you say it, everybody is a manifestation of the divine, playing this game and that game. Your not knowing it, if you do not know it, is part of the game. It makes it all the more fun. "Get lost," you say to yourself, and lost you get.

We all like to go to a horror movie and have the cold shivers because we think something awful is going to happen, something is going to be seen on the screen that we cannot stand to see. We all expose ourselves to thrills like that. Children and young people expose themselves to dreadful things. Their parents get the heebie-jeebies. If it isn't getting drunk or driving hot rods, they take drugs that may ruin their sanity for life. If they do not take drugs, they do something else to see how close to the point of danger they can get. Most people who go in for racing cars usually end up crashing. Life is geared to being played dangerously. I would say to those among you who are the most ignorant, unspiritual, and stuffy, Congratulations! You are so lost in the game you do not even know where you stand, and are taking a gorgeous risk. Because of you we might even blow up the planet, and how close are we going to get with that one? In the same way as that car racer watches the speedometer needle going up, up, and up, there are people feeling more and more self-righteously determined that good shall prevail in the world, all the while watching the needle of world tension go up. It is getting hotter and hotter and hotter, and finally we may all go out in a blaze of glory. When the dust settles they will say, "That was quite a dream we have just woken up from. What shall we do next?"

That is why I say that my function is that of a liberator. I want you to see that it is you, not me, not Swami So-and-so, not Buddha So-and-so, not Saint So-and-so who is responsible, it is you. Sir Edwin Arnold put these words into the mouth of the Buddha: "You suffer from yourselves. No one else compels you to live and die and whirl upon the wheel and hug and kiss its spokes of agony, its tire of tears, its nave of nothingness."

One of the old Zen masters went to his teacher and said, "What is the way to liberation?"

The teacher said, "Who is restraining you?"

He answered, "No one."

"If so," his teacher asked, "why need you ask for liberation?"

It all bounces back to you. What do you want? Do you know what you want? Think it through and say exactly what you want. Invariably you will get back to where you are. It is all happening because you are doing it. Why meditate, then? Why do anything of a so-called spiritual nature?

People do not really understand what meditation is. Meditation is the one human activity that has no purpose. Buddhists who are supposed to have attained everything are invariably shown in some sort of meditation posture. Why should they meditate anymore? Because that just happens to be the way a Buddhist sits. When he sits, he sits. When he walks, he walks. He is not going anywhere. He is just going for a walk because he digs it. The very word *dig* means not merely to appreciate, but to penetrate, to go to the heart of the matter, to penetrate the moment. To get to the root of the moment is to get to the center of you. Where you are is where you start, where you begin all this questioning. Where does the question and the desire spring from? That is you, and that you is the point from which the whole universe is created, flowing back into the past like the wake of a ship. The wake does not drive the ship, it is the ship that makes the wake. Meditation is just sitting and watching it happen. It is not done because it is good for you. It is done for fun. Meditation is an enjoyable thing. If it is not, you are not really meditating.

There is an awful game that meditators play, which is competitive suffering. They go to some place where they sit for hours on end, until their legs ache and practically fall off. Then they come back and brag about sitting through all those hours of leg ache. It is very difficult to put down people who are suffering. One has a natural sympathy for pain, but I sometimes want to say, "For goodness sake, do not throw your suffering at me in that way and in that spirit. Do not brag about it. Do not one-up me by saying you have suffered more than I have." People say many things like, "I am more aware of my shortcomings than you are." "I am more tolerant than you are." "I recognize more than you what a rascal I am." There are many kinds of ways of one-upping somebody else in order to play the game in which you always win. Once we get into that kind of thing with meditation, we get into hierarchies, ranks, and degrees, and end up by asking, "Who has attained level seven, who has attained level nine?"

The expert guru will always set you a stage higher than you have ever thought of, in order to see how far your ambition will run. This goes on endlessly, endlessly, endlessly, until you suddenly wake up and begin real meditation, by realizing that you are there, that you really do meditate all the time just by virtue of existing all the time.

NOT WHAT SHOULD BE, BUT WHAT IS!

CHAPTER TWO

I wonder what is meant when we use the word *I*. I have been very interested in this problem, and have come to the conclusion that what most civilized people mean by that word is a hallucination, a false sense of personal identity that is at complete variance with the facts of nature. As a result of having a false sense of identity, we act in a way that is inappropriate to our natural environment, and when that inappropriate way of action is magnified by a very powerful technology, we see a profound discord begin to separate man and nature. As is well known, we are now in the process of destroying our environment as a result of an attempt to conquer it and master it. We believe that our environment is something other than ourselves, and in assuming that, we make a great mistake and are now paying the price.

Most people would agree with the lines of the poet who said, "I, a stranger and afraid in a world I never made." We have the strong sensation that the being inside our skin is extremely different from the world outside our skin. We believe that while there may be intelligence and values and loving feelings inside human skins, outside them is a world of mechanical process that does not give a damn about any individual. We believe the physical world is a result of unintelligent gyrations of blind forces, while the biological world consists merely of gyrations of libido, Freud's word for blind lust. There are many people who say they do not believe that the world is like that, but is under the control of a wise, just, and beneficent God. Although many people say they believe that to be the case, very few in fact, actually do. A great many think that they ought to believe in God, but they actually do not, because the idea of God, as handed down in popular Christianity, Judaism, and Islam, has become implausible to most educated people. They would love to believe it, but they cannot. What was avant-garde thinking in the eighteenth and nineteenth centuries in the West—that the universe is a machine—has become the common sense of the average person of today. Most people have not caught up in their common sense with the universe of modern physics. We still think about the world in Newtonian categories, not in the categories of quantum theory.

Psychoanalysis, for example, is a Newtonian conception of our psychological mechanisms—and notice that we speak of unconscious mental mechanisms. We think of the libido in the same way as Ernst Hekel thought of the energy of the universe as blind or unconscious. Psychoanalysis is in a sense psychohydraulics, because of its analogy between psychic energy and the flow of water. In all this, the view of the nineteenth century is that the human psyche—the mind, the ego, the superego, the id—is all basically a mechanical functioning.

The nineteenth century strove to take an objective attitude to nature and to be the very opposite of what we presume to call "primitive" animism, the point of view that sees everything as alive, held by people who converse with animals, plants, rivers, mountains, and stars. Thinkers of the nineteenth century said that this is the pathetic fallacy, a projection of intelligent human characteristics on unintelligent entities in nature. We withdrew that projection in the nineteenth century and said, "Let us look at everything objectively, as it is." Then we turned that attitude on ourselves, and studied human physiology and human psychology as objects. However, when we discovered ourselves to be objects, we decided that the time had come for suicide, because all objects, as the name implies, are of course objectionable. I found that phrase, which I thought I had invented myself, in the writings of Weston La Barre, who is a great anthropologist, but definitely of the psychoanalytic school that shares this nineteenth-century philosophy of so-called scientific naturalism. He uses the phrase, "the objectionable, objective world." So when everything is deprived of subjectivity and is regarded as simply a mechanism, with nobody home as it were, then the world is seen as futile. And indeed we are preparing to destroy the planet with nuclear energy, and other processes.

I submit that this nineteenth-century view of the world is pure mythology, and not very good mythology at that. It is fundamentally based on the hallucination that we have about our own existence. It should be obvious that the human being goes with the rest of the universe, even though we say in popular speech, "I came into this world." It is not true that you came into this world. You came out of it, in the same way as a flower comes out of a plant, or a fruit comes out of a tree. An apple tree apples, the solar system—and therefore the galaxy, and therefore the whole system of galaxies in which we live—that system peoples. People, therefore, are an expression of its energy and of its nature.

If people are intelligent, and I suppose we have to grant that, then the energy that people express must also be intelligent, because one does not gather figs from thistles, or grapes from thorns. But it does not occur to ordinary, civilized people to regard themselves as expressions of the whole universe. It should be obvious that we cannot exist except in an environment of earth, air, water, and mild temperature, and that all these things go with us and are as important to us—albeit outside our skins—as our internal organs, our stomachs, and our brains.

If we cannot describe the behavior of organisms without at the same time describing the behavior of their environments, we should realize that we have a new entity of description. It is not the individual organism alone but a "field of behavior," which we must call, rather clumsily, the organism/environment. You go with your environment in the same way as your head goes with the rest of your body. However, it is not this way when we think of a person. If you suddenly think of your mother, what you think of is her face. We are used to representing people in the newspapers, magazines, books, and in art galleries with a head-and-shoulders portrait. We think of the feet, the legs, the back of the torso, as all somehow irrelevant. Here is a truncated face, and that is the person. So we say, "Put a good face on it," and endeavor to save face, to preserve the front.

Oddly enough, the very word *person* is in Latin *persona,* that through which sound passes. It refers to the megaphone mask worn by actors in Greco-Roman drama. The dramatis personae, the list of the characters to appear in the play, was originally the list of masks that were to be worn. Therefore your person, your personality, is your mask. So the question is, What is behind the mask? Notice that the whole body goes with this face. You do not find in nature faces arriving in the world sui generis; they go with a body. Also, bodies do not arrive on a plain ball of scrubbed rock floating without an atmosphere far away from a star. That world would not grow bodies. There would be no soil for bodies. There would be no body-producing complexity of environment. Bodies go with a very complicated natural environment. And if the head goes with the body, and the body goes with the environment, then the body is as much an integral part of the environment as the head is part of the body. It is deceptive, of course, because the human being is not rooted to the ground like a tree. A human being moves about, and can therefore shift from one environment to another. However, these shifts are superficial. The basic environment of the planet remains a constant, and if the human being leaves the planet, they have to take with them a canned version of the planetary environment.

We are not really aware of this relationship. On taking thought and due consideration it does occur to us that, yes, indeed, we do need that environment, but ordinarily we do not feel it. That is to say, we do not have a vivid sensation of belonging to our environment in the same way that we have a vivid sensation of being an ego inside a bag of skin, located about halfway between the ears and a little way behind the eyes. Since we feel the ego that way, and that is not the way we really exist, I call the "I" a hallucination. So, today we live with the disastrous results of the ego, which, according to nineteenth-century common sense, feels that it is a fluke in nature and that if it does not fight nature it will not be able to maintain its status as an intelligent fluke. Therefore the geneticists and many others are now saying that man must take the course of his evolution into his own hands. He can no longer trust the wiggly, random, unintelligible processes of nature to develop him any further; he must intercede with his own intelligence and through genetic alterations breed the kind of people who will be viable for future human societies. This, I submit, is a ghastly error, because human intelligence has a very serious limitation. It is a scanning system of conscious attention that is linear, and it examines the world in lines, rather as you would pass the beam of a flashlight or a spotlight across a room. The reason our education takes so long is that we have to scan miles of lines of print, and we regard that as essential information. However, the universe does not come at us in lines. Instead, it comes at us in a multidimensional continuum in which everything is happening altogether everywhere at once, and it comes at us much too quickly to be translated into lines of print or other information, however fast it may be scanned. That is our limitation, so far as the intellectual and scientific life is concerned. The computer may greatly speed up linear scanning, but it is still linear scanning.

So long as we are stuck with that linear form of wisdom, we cannot deal with more than a few variables at once. Now, what do I mean by that? A variable is any one linear process. Let us take music. When you play a Bach fugue, and there are four parts to it, you have four variables. You have four moving lines, and you can take care of that with two hands. An organist using two feet can put in two more variables and have six going. You may realize, if you have ever tried to play the organ, that it is quite difficult to make six independent motions go at once. The average person cannot do that without training. In fact, the average person cannot deal with more than three variables at once without using a pencil.

When we study physics, we are dealing with processes in which there are millions of variables. However, we handle this problem with statistics, in the same way as insurance companies use actuarial tables to predict when most people will die. However, if the average age of death is sixty-five, this average does not apply to any given individual. Any given individual will live to an individual age, and the range of individual ages at death may be very wide indeed. But that is all right, because the sixty-five guess works when you are doing large-scale gambling. In a similar way, the physicist is able to predict the behavior of nuclear wavicles. But the practical problems of human life deal with variables in the hundreds of thousands. Here statistical methods are very poor, and reaching accurate conclusions by linear means is impossible.

Now then, with such limited equipment we are proposing to interfere with our genes, and with that equipment we are trying to solve our political, economic, and social problems. Naturally, everybody has a sense of total frustration and asks, "What on earth can I do?" We do not seem to know a way of calling on our brains. This is unfortunate because our brains can handle an enormous number of variables that are not accessible to conscious attention. Your brain and your total nervous system are now handling your blood chemistry, the secretions from your glands, the behavior of millions of cells. It is doing all that without thinking about it, without translating the processes it is handling into consciously reviewed words, symbols, or numbers. When I use the word *thinking,* I mean precisely that process of translating what is going on in nature into words, symbols, or numbers. Of course, both words and numbers are kinds of symbols. Symbols bear the same relation to the real world that money bears to wealth. You cannot quench anybody's thirst with the word *water,* just as you cannot eat a dollar bill and derive nutrition from it. But scanning, using symbols and using conscious intelligence, has proved very useful to us. It has given us such technology as we have; but at the same time, it has proved too much of a good thing. We have become so fascinated with it that we confuse the world as it is with the world as it is thought about, talked about, and figured about—the world as it is described. The difference between these two is vast, and when we are not aware of ourselves except in a symbolic way, we are not related to ourselves at all, and that is why we all feel psychologically frustrated.

Thus we come back to the question of what we mean by "I." First of all, obviously we mean our symbol of ourselves. Ourselves, in this case, is the whole psychophysical organism, conscious and unconscious, plus its environment. That is your real self. In other words, your real self is the universe as centered on your organism—that is you! Now, allow me to clarify that just a little. What you do is also a doing of your environment. Your behavior is its behavior, as much as its behavior is your behavior. It is mutual. We could say it is transactional. You are not a puppet that your environment pushes around, nor is the environment a puppet that you push around. They go together, and they act together—in the same way, for example, one side of a wheel is going down as the other side of it is going up. When you turn the steering wheel of a car, are you pulling it or are you pushing it? You are doing both, aren't you? When you pull it down one side, you are pushing it up on the other. It is all one, and in the same way there is a push-pull between organism and environment.

We are only rarely aware of this in curious alterations of consciousness that we call mystical experiences or cosmic consciousness, when an individual gets the feeling that everything that is happening is of his own doing. Or it could be the opposite of that feeling, that they are not doing anything, but that all their doings, their decisions and so forth, are happenings of nature. You can feel it either way, and you can describe it in these two completely opposite ways, but you are talking about the same experience. You are talking about experiencing your own activity and the activity of nature as one single process. You can describe it as if you were omnipotent, like God, or as if it were completely deterministic and you hardly existed at all. But remember, both points of view are right, and we will see where that gets us.

We do not feel that ordinarily, do we? What we feel, instead, is an identification of ourselves with our idea of ourselves—I would rather say, with our image of ourselves. That is the person, or the ego. You play a role; you identify with that role. I play a role called Alan Watts. And I know very well that it is a big act. I can play some other roles besides Alan Watts if necessary, but I find this one is best for making a living. But I assure you that is a mask and I do not take it seriously. The idea of my being a kind of guru, or savior of the world just breaks me up, because I know me. Besides, it is very difficult to be holy, in the ordinary sense.

So, I know I am not that, but most of us are taught

to think that we are whom we are called. When you are a little child and you begin to learn a role, your parents and your peers approve of your being that. In that way they know who you are. You are predictable, so you can be controlled. However, when you act out of role and you imitate some other child's behavior, everybody points the finger and says, "You are not being true to yourself. Johnny, that's not you, that's Peter." So you learn to stay Johnny, not Peter. But, of course, you are not either, because these are just images of you. They are as much of you as you can get into your conscious attention, which is precious little.

Your image of yourself contains no information about how you structure your nervous system. It contains no information about your blood chemistry. It contains almost no information about the subtle influences of society on your behavior. It also does not include the basic assumptions of your culture, which are all taken for granted and unconscious. You cannot make them conscious unless you study other cultures to see how their basic assumptions differ. Your self-image includes all kinds of illusions of which you are completely unaware, for example, that time is real and that there is such a thing as a past, which is pure conjecture. Nevertheless, all these things are unconscious in us, and they are not included in our image of ourselves, nor is there any information included in our image of ourselves about our inseparable relationships with the whole natural universe. In all this is a very impoverished image.

When you ask a person, "What did you do yesterday?" they will give you a historical account of a certain number of events in which they participated, and a certain number of things that they saw, used, or were clobbered by. You will realize at once that this history leaves out most of what happens. If I try to describe what happens to me this evening, I will never be able to describe it, because there are so many people here that if I were to talk about everyone whom I have seen, what they were wearing, what color their hair was, and what sort of expressions they had on their faces, I would have to talk until doomsday. So instead of this rich physical experience, which is very rich indeed, I have to attenuate it in memory and description and say, "I met a lot of people in Philadelphia. There were men and there were women; lots of them were young and some of them were old." Now this is an utterly impoverished account of what went on. Therefore, in thinking of ourselves in this way—in terms of this stringy, mangy account, of what I did yesterday, and the day before—all I have is a caricature of myself. Of course a caricature does not really draw us in, but just puts on certain salient features whereby people can recognize you. It's a sort of skeleton, and in this way we are conceiving of ourselves as a bunch of skeletons. They have no flesh on them, and just a bunch of bones.

It is no wonder we all feel inadequate. We are all looking for something in the future to bring us a golden goodie at the end of the line somewhere. We hope that there is a good time coming—be it ever so far away—some far-off, divine event to which all creation moves. Therefore, when we say of something that it is no good, we mean "It has no future." I would say, "It has no present." When everybody says "It has no future," that is plainly ridiculous.

As a result, we are psychically starved and therefore always looking, and seeking. This confused seeking is going on everywhere because we do not know what we want. Nobody really knows what they want. Instead we think of what we want in vague terms of pleasure, money, wealth, love, fulfillment, or personal development. However, we do not know what we mean by all of that.

If a person really sits down to write a twenty-page essay on their idea of heaven, it will inevitably be a sorry production. This can be seen in medieval art, where we find depictions of heaven and hell. Hell is always much better than heaven, and although it is uncomfortable, it is a sadomasochistic orgy. Hell is really rip-roaring, whereas all the saints in heaven are sitting smugly as if they were in church. Looking down you can see all the heads of the multitudes of the saved, which the artist has drawn to abbreviate them. They look like cobblestone streets.

What has happened is that our eye has been trained to see an illusion. It is merely an image, and it is no more ourself than an idol is the Godhead. Yet we say, "That cannot be so, because I feel I really exist. It is not just an idea in my head. It is a feeling; I feel me." However, what is it that you feel when you feel "I"? I will tell you. What is the difference between looking at something and taking a hard look at it, or hearing something and listening intently? What is the difference between waiting while something goes on, and enduring it? The difference is that when you pay attention, instead of just looking, you screw up your face. You frown and stare in a futile muscular activity. When you listen intently, you start by doing some face squeezing, then you grit your teeth, or clench your fists. When you endure, you pull yourself together physically, and therefore you sit upright. You hold your breath. You do all kinds of muscular things to control the functioning of your nervous system, and none of them have the slightest effect on its proper operation. If you stare at things, you may fuzz the image rather than seeing it clearly. If you listen intently by concentrating on muscles around the ears, you will be attending to your muscles so much that you may not hear things properly. If you tighten up your body to pull yourself together, all you accomplish is to constrict yourself.

I remember sitting next to a boy in school who had great difficulty in learning to read. Teachers always say to children, "Try. If you cannot do it, you must try." So the boy tried, and when he was trying to get out words he grunted and groaned as if he were lifting weights. The teacher was impressed because the boy was really trying. The boy got a B for effort, but all he was doing was straining uselessly. We all make this muscular strain in the belief that it is achieving the sort of psychological results we intended to achieve. But this is like taking off in a jet plane, and when you get a mile down the runway and the plane is not up in the air yet, you begin to get nervous. So you start pulling at your seat belt. That is symptomatic of the chronic feeling we have in us all the time that corresponds to the word *I*.

When you see yourself as "I," you feel that chronic tension. In much the same way when an organ is working properly, you do not feel it. If you see your eye, you may have cataracts. If you hear your ears, you have ringing in your ears getting in the way of hearing. When you are fully functioning you are unaware of the body. When you are thinking clearly, your brain is not getting in your way. Of course, you are seeing your eyes in the sense that everything you see out in front of you is a condition in the optic nerves at the back of the skull. That is where you are aware of all this, but you are not aware of the eye as the eye, the optical eye. When we are aware of the ego as "I," we are aware of a chronic tension inside ourselves, and that is not us. It is just a futile tension. And then we wonder why "I" cannot do anything, why "I" feel impotent in the face of all the problems of the world, and why "I" somehow cannot manage to transform "I." Here we come to the real problem, because we are always telling each other that we should be different. However, I am not going to tell you that because I know that you cannot be different, nor can I. That may sound depressing, but I will show you that it is not. It is actually very heartening. Everybody who is at all sensitive and awake to their own problems, and humanity's problems, is trying to change themselves. We know we cannot change the world unless we change ourselves. If we are all individually selfish, we are going to be collectively selfish. As it is said in the Bible, "Thou shalt love the Lord thy God, and love your neighbor as yourself." We all agree that we must love, but we do not, and this becomes particularly appalling when we enter into the higher realm of spiritual development.

Everybody these days is interested in spiritual development, and wisely so, because we want to change our consciousness. Many people are well aware that this egocentric consciousness is a hallucination, and they presume it is the function of religion to change it. After all, that is what the Zen Buddhists, and all these yogis in the Orient are doing. They are changing their state of consciousness to get something called satori, or mystical experience, or nirvana, or moksha.

Everybody is really enthused about that because it is the definitive spiritual experience, and you do not get that in church. Although there have been Christian mystics, the church has been very quiet about them. In the average church, all you get is talk—there is no meditation and no spiritual discipline. They interminably tell God what to do, as if He did not know. Then they tell the people what to do, as if they could do what they're told, or even wanted to. Then they sing religious nursery rhymes. And then, to cap it all, the Roman Catholic Church—which at least had an unintelligible service that was real mysterious and suggested vast goings-on—went on to put the service into bad English. They took away incense, and became essentially a bunch of Protestants, and so now even the Catholics are at loose ends. As Clare Boothe Luce said, "It is no longer possible to practice contemplative prayer at mass." You are being advised, exhorted, and edified all the time, and that becomes a bore. Think of God, listening to all those prayers. Talk about grieving the Holy Spirit. It is just awful; people have no consideration for God at all.

In pursuing spiritual disciplines, however, such as yoga, Zen, and also psychotherapy, there arises a difficulty. This difficulty lies in wanting to find a method whereby I can change my consciousness and improve myself. But the self that needs to be improved is the one that is doing the improving, and so I am rather stuck. I find out that the reason I think I believe in God is that I hope that somehow God will rescue me. In other words, I want to hang on to my own existence and feel rather shaky about doing that for myself, so I hope there is a God who will take care of it. Or I may think that if only I could be loving, I would have a better opinion of myself. I could face myself if I were more loving. So by some gimmickry the unloving me has to turn itself into a loving me. This is just like trying to lift yourself off the ground with your own bootstraps; it cannot be done. That is why religion, in practice, mainly produces hypocrisy and guilt, due to the constant failure of these enterprises.

People study Zen, and they say that getting rid of your ego is a superhuman task. I assure you it is very, very difficult to get rid of your ego. You have to sit for a long time, and you are going to get the sorest legs. It is hard work, and all you wretched kids who think you are getting rid of your ego with easy yoga do not know what you are in for. The biggest ego trip is getting rid of your

33

ego, and of course the joke of it all is that your ego does not exist. There is nothing to get rid of. It is an illusion, as I have tried to explain, but still you ask how to stop the illusion. But who is asking? In the ordinary sense in which we use the word *I*, how can I stop identifying myself with the wrong me? The answer is simply that you cannot.

The Christians acknowledge this by saying that mystical experience is a gift of divine grace. Man, as such, cannot achieve this experience; it is a gift of God, and if God does not give it to you there is no way of getting it. That is solidly true, since you cannot do anything about it because you do not exist. You might say that is pretty depressing news, but the whole point is that it is not depressing news. It is the joyous news. There is a Zen poem that talks about "it," meaning the mystical experience, satori, the realization that you are, as Jesus was, the eternal energy of the universe. The poem says, "You cannot catch hold of it, nor can you get rid of it. In not being able to get it, you get it. When you speak, it is silent. When you are silent, it speaks."

This phrase—not being able to get it, you get it—is the feeling Krishnamurti tries to convey to people when he says, "Why do you ask for a method? There is no method. All methods are simply gimmicks for strengthening your ego." How do we not ask for a method? He answers, "In asking that you are still asking for a method." There is no method. If you really understand what your "I" is, you will see there is no method. We think this is so sad, but it is not. This is the gospel, the good news, because if you cannot achieve it, if you cannot transform yourself, that means that the main obstacle to mystical vision has collapsed. That obstacle was you. What happens next? By now you are at your wit's end, but what are you going to do—commit suicide?

Suppose you just put that off for a little while, and wait and see what happens. You cannot control your thoughts, and you cannot control your feelings, because there is no controller. You are your thoughts and your feelings, and they are running along, running along, running along. Just sit and watch them. There they go. You are still breathing, aren't you? Still growing your hair; still seeing and hearing. Are you doing that? Is breathing something that you do? Do you see? Do you organize the operations of your eyes, and know exactly how to work those rods and cones in the retina? Do you do that? It happens, and it is a happening. Your breathing is happening. Your thinking is happening. Your feeling is happening. Your hearing, your seeing, the clouds are happening across the sky. The sky is happening blue; the sun is happening shining. There it is: all this happening.

May I introduce you? This is yourself. This is a vision of who you really are, and the way you really function. You function by happening, that is to say, by spontaneous occurrence. This is not a state of affairs that you should realize. I cannot possibly preach about it to you, because the minute you start thinking "I should understand that," the stupid notion that "I" should bring it about arises again, when there is no "you" to bring it about. That is why I am not preaching. You can only preach to egos. All I can do is talk about what is. It amuses me to talk about what is because it is wonderful. I love it, and therefore I like to talk about it. If I get paid for it, it is because sensible people get paid for doing what they enjoy doing. My whole approach is not to convert you, not to make you over, not to improve you, but for you to discover that if you really knew the way you were, things would be sane. However, you cannot do that. You cannot make that discovery because you are in your own way so long as you think "I" am "I," so long as that hallucination blocks it. The hallucination disappears only in the realization of its own futility, when at last you see that you cannot make yourself over.

A lot of yoga teachers may try to get you to control your own mind, mainly to prove to you that you cannot do it. "A fool who persists in his folly will become wise," and so they speed up the folly. Initially you may have a certain amount of superficial success by a process commonly called self-hypnosis, and you may think you are making progress. A good teacher will let you go along that way for a while, until he really throws you by asking, "Why are you concentrating?"

Buddhism works very much in this way. Buddha said, "If you suffer, you suffer because you desire, and your desires are either unattainable or always disappointed. So cut out desire." So those disciples went away and they stamped on desire, jumped on desire, cut the throat of desire, and threw out desire. When they came back, Buddha said, "But you are still desiring not to desire." They wondered how to get rid of that desire. When you see that all of this is nonsense, there naturally comes over you a quietness. Seeing that you cannot control your mind, you realize there is no controller. What you took to be the thinker of thoughts is just one of the thoughts. What you took to be the feeler of the feelings is just one of the feelings. What you took to be the experiencer of experience is just a part of the experience.

There is not any thinker of thoughts or feeler of feelings. We get into that bind because our language has a grammatical rule that states that verbs must have subjects. The funny thing about this is that verbs are processes, and so are subjects and nouns, which are supposed to be things. How does a noun start a verb? How does a thing put a process into action? Obviously it cannot, but we always insist that there is this subject called the knower, and without a knower there cannot be knowing. However, that is just a grammatical rule, not a rule of nature. In nature there is just knowing. If you say that you are feeling, it is as if you were somehow different from the feeling. When I say "I am feeling," what I mean is, there is feeling here. When I say "You are feeling," I mean there is feeling there.

Some years ago I had just given a talk on television when one of the announcers came up to me and said, "If one can believe that this universe is in the charge of an intelligent and beneficent God, don't you think He would naturally have provided us with an infallible guide to behavior and to the truth about the universe?" Of course I knew he meant the Bible, and so I said, "No, I think nothing of the kind, because I think a loving God would not do something to His children that would rot their brains." If we had an infallible guide we would never think for ourselves, and therefore our minds would become atrophied. It is as if my grandfather had left me a million dollars, and I am glad he didn't. Therefore we have to begin any discussion of the meaning of the life and teachings of Jesus with a look at this thorny question of authority, and especially the authority of Holy Scripture.

In this country in particular there are an enormous number of people who seem to believe that the Bible descended from heaven with an angel in the year 1611, which was when the so-called King James, or more correctly, the Authorized Version of the Bible was translated into English. I had a crazy uncle who believed that every word of the Bible was literally true, including the marginal notes. Whatever date it said in the marginal notes—for instance, that the world was created in 4004 B.C.—he believed as the word of God. One day he was reading a passage in the Book of Proverbs and found a naughty word, and from that time on he was through with it. How Protestant can you get?

The question of authority needs to be understood because I am not going to claim any authority in what I say to you except the authority, such as it is, of history. Of course, that is a pretty uncertain authority, but from my point of view the four Gospels are to be regarded, on the whole, as historical documents. I will even grant the miracles because speaking as one heavily influenced by Buddhism, I do not find miracles particularly impressive. The traditions of Asia—Hindu, Buddhist, Taoist, and so forth—are full of miraculous stories. We take them in our stride and don't think they are signs of anything in particular except psychic power. Of course, we in the West have, by scientific technology, accomplished things of a very startling nature. We could blow up the whole planet, and even Tibetan magicians have never promised to do anything like that. I am really a little scared of the growing interest in psychic power, which I call psychotechnics. We have made such a mess of things with ordinary technics that heaven only knows what we might do if we got hold of psychotechnics and started raising people from the dead and prolonging life insufferably and doing everything we wished.

In the whole, the idea of miracles is simply this: Imagine that you are God and that you can have anything you want. After a while you would say, "This is getting pretty dull because I know in advance everything that is going to happen." So you would wish for a surprise, and you would find yourself this evening in this church as a human being. I think miracles are probably possible. Miracles do not bother me, and as a matter of fact, when you read the writings of the early fathers of the church, the great theologians like Saint Clement, Gregory of Nyssa, Saint John of Damascus, and even Saint Thomas Aquinas, are not interested in the historicity of the Bible. They take miracles for granted, and forget about it. They are interested in a deeper meaning. Therefore they see in the story of Jonah and the whale a prefiguration of the resurrection of Christ. Even when it comes to the resurrection of Christ they are not worrying about the chemistry or the physics of a risen body. What they are interested in is that the idea of the resurrection of the body has something to say about the meaning of the physical body in the eyes of God. They have discovered that the physical body, in other words, is not something worthless and unspiritual but something that is an object of the Divine Love. Therefore, I am not going to be concerned with whether or not miraculous events happen. That seems to me entirely beside the point.

I regard the four Gospels, including the Gospel of John, as, on the whole, as good a historical document as anything we have from that period, and that is important. It used to be fashionable to regard the Gospel of

John as late. At the turn of the century, the higher critics of the New Testament assigned the Gospel of John to about 125 A.D., and the reason was simple. Those higher critics just assumed that the basic teachings of Jesus could not possibly have included any complicated mystical theology. Therefore they said, "It must be from a later time." But as a matter of fact, in the text of the Gospel of John, the topography of Jerusalem and the references to the Jewish calendar are more accurate than those in any of the other three books, Matthew, Mark, and Luke. Therefore it seems to me perfectly simple to assume that John recorded the inner teachings that Jesus gave to his disciples, and that Matthew, Mark, and Luke recorded the more exoteric teaching, which he gave to people at large.

Now, what about the authority of these Scriptures? A lot of people do not know how we got the Bible at all. We in the West got it thanks to the Catholic Church. The Catholic Church and members of the church wrote the books of the New Testament, and they took over the books of the Old Testament. So it was the Catholic Church that promulgated the Bible and said, "We give you these Scriptures on our authority, and by the authority of the informal tradition that has existed among us from the beginning, inspired by the Holy Spirit." So, historically, we have received the Bible on the church's say-so.

The Catholic Church insists, therefore, that it, speaking collectively under the presumed guidance of the Holy Spirit, has the authority to interpret the Bible, and you can take that or leave it. Obviously the authority of the Bible is not, first of all, based on the Bible itself. I can write a bible and state within that book that it is indeed the word of God that I have received, and you are at liberty to believe me or not. Hindus believe that the Vedas are divinely revealed, and they are inspired with just as much fervor as any Christian or any Jew. Muslims believe that the Koran is divinely inspired, and some Buddhists believe that their sutras are also of divine, or rather, Buddhistic origin. The Japanese believe that the ancient texts of Shinto are likewise of divine origin. And who is to judge? If we are going to argue about which version of the truth is the correct one, we will always end up in a dispute in which the judge and the advocate are the same person, and you would not want that if you were brought into a court of law. If I were to say that I find Jesus Christ to be the greatest being who ever came onto this earth, by what standards do I judge? Why, obviously, I will judge by the sort of moral standards that have been given to me as somebody brought up in a Christian culture. There is nobody impartial who can decide between all the religions because everybody has been, in one way or another, influenced by one of them. So, if the church says the Bible is true, it finally comes back to you. Are you going to believe the church or aren't you? If nobody believes the church, it will be perfectly plain that the church has no authority, because the people are always the source of authority. That is why Tocqueville said that people get the government they deserve.

You may say, "God Himself has the authority." Well, how are we to show that? That is your opinion. So you say, "You wait and see. The Day of Judgment is coming, and then you will find out who is the authority." Yes, but at the moment there is no evidence for the Day of Judgment. It remains simply your opinion that the Day of Judgment is coming. There is nothing else to go on except the opinion of other people, whose opinion you buy. Really, I will not deny anybody's right to hold these opinions. You may indeed believe that the Bible is literally true and that it was actually dictated by God to Moses and the prophets and the apostles. That may be your opinion and you are at liberty to hold it.

However, I do not agree with you. I do believe, on the other hand, that there is a sense in which the Bible is divinely inspired. However, I mean by inspiration something utterly different from receiving a dictated message from an omniscient authority. I think inspiration comes very seldom in words. In fact, almost all the words written down by automatic writing from psychic input that I have read strike me as rather thin. When psychics write of deep mysteries—instead of telling you what your sickness is or who your grandmother was—they become superficial. Psychically communicated philosophy is never as interesting as philosophy carefully thought out.

Divine inspiration is not that kind of verbal or psychic communication anyway. An example of divine inspiration is the feeling that, for reasons you cannot understand, you love people. Divine inspiration is wisdom, which is very difficult to put into words. It is a mystical experience. A person who writes out of that experience could be said to be divinely inspired. Inspiration might come through dreams, or through archetypal messages from the collective unconscious, through which the Holy Spirit could be said to work. But since inspiration is always conveyed through a human vehicle, it is liable to be distorted by that vehicle. I am talking to you through a sound system, but if there is something wrong with it, whatever truths I might utter to you will be distorted. My voice will be distorted, and you might mistake the meaning of what I say. Similarly, anybody who receives divine inspiration will express it through the language they know. By language I do not only mean English, Latin, Greek, Hebrew, or Sanskrit. I mean language in the sense of the sort of concepts that are available to you, for invariably you will express yourself through the concepts of the religion you were brought up with.

Now suppose you were brought up in the Bible Belt. If that was all you knew of religion, and you had a mystical experience of the type where you suddenly discovered that you are one with God, you would be liable to get up and say, "I am Jesus Christ." However, the culture that we live in just cannot allow that. People would say, "You don't look like you're Jesus Christ coming back again, because it says in the Scripture that when he comes back, he will appear in the heavens with legions of angels, and you are not doing that. You are just the same old Joe Dokes that we knew years ago, and now you're saying you are Jesus Christ." "Well," Joe Dokes says, "when Jesus Christ said he was God, nobody believed him, either." But Jesus said he was God because he was trying to express what had happened to him in terms of a religious language that was circumscribed by the Holy Bible. He had never read the Upanishads. He had never read the *Diamond Sutra*. He had never read the Tibetan Book of the Dead or the *I Ching* or Lao-tzu. But if he and the culture, the society in which he was talking, had read the Upanishads, they would have had no difficulty with his claim to being God. Because it says in the Upanishads, we are all incarnations of God; although, it is true, they do not mean the same thing that a Hebrew meant by God, and of course they do not use that word, they use the word *Brahman*. The Brahman is neither personal nor impersonal. I would say Brahman is suprapersonal. Brahman is not he or she. Brahman is not the creator of the world—as a thing underneath and subject to Brahman—but is the actor of the world, the player of all the parts. Like an absorbed actor, the divine spirit gets so involved in playing the role as to become bewitched. This is all part of the game, to be bewitched into believing "I am that role."

When you were babies you knew who you were, and psychoanalysts refer to that as the oceanic feeling. They do not really like it, but they admit that the baby cannot distinguish between the world and the way it acts on the world. It is all one process, which is of course the way things are. But we are taught very quickly those things that are you and those that are not. We learn very quickly what is voluntary and what is involuntary, because you can be punished for the voluntary but not for the involuntary. So, we unlearn what we knew in the beginning. And in the course of life, if we are fortunate, we discover again what we really are, that each one of us is what would be called in Arabic, or Hebrew, the Son of God. The phrase "Son of" means "of the nature of," as when you call someone a "son of a bitch." So, "Son of God" means a divine person, a human being who is in the nature of God and realizes it.

My assumption or opinion is that Jesus of Nazareth was a human being, like Buddha, Shri Ramakrishna, Ramana Maharshi who, early in life had colossal experiences of what we call cosmic consciousness. Now you do not have to be of any particular kind of religion to get this experience. It can hit anyone, anytime, like falling in love. There are obviously a number of you in this building who have had it in greater or lesser degree, but it is found all over the world, and when it hits you, you know it. Sometimes it comes after long practice of meditation and spiritual discipline, and sometimes it comes for no reason that anybody can determine. We say it is the grace of God, and with this there comes an overwhelming conviction that you have mistaken your identity. I'm not just old Alan Watts—that was completely superficial. Instead I find I am an expression of an eternal something or other, a name that cannot be named, as the name of God was taboo among the Hebrews. I am, and I suddenly understand exactly why everything is the way it is. It is perfectly clear. Furthermore, I no longer feel any boundary between what I do and what happens to me. I feel that everything that is going on is my doing, just as my breathing is. Do you do it or does it happen to you? You can feel it both ways. There is just this great happening going on. If you have the name in your background you will say that this happening is God, or the will of God, or the doing of God. If you do not have that word in your background, you might say with the Chinese, "It is the flowing of the Tao." Or if you are a Hindu, you will say, "It is the maya of Brahman." *Maya* means the magical power, the creative illusion, the play.

You can very well understand how people to whom this happens feel genuinely inspired. Very often there goes along with it an extremely warm feeling, because you see the divine in everybody else's eyes. When the great Hindu-Muslim mystic Kabir was a very old man, he used to look around at people and say, "To whom shall I preach?" He could see the beloved in all eyes. Sometimes I look into people's eyes and see that same beloved in the depth of those pools, and yet the expression on the face around those eyes is saying, "Who, me?" It is the funniest thing, but everybody is playing out an essential part in this colossal cosmic drama. Yet, the presence of the beloved is so pervasive that you can even feel it in people you thoroughly dislike.

So let us suppose that Jesus had such an experience. These experiences are of all ranges, as I have said, and his could have been a very strong one indeed. From the sayings of Jesus, especially in the Gospel of John, anybody who studied the psychology of religion can easily detect that that experience must have taken place, or something very like it. However, Jesus had a limitation, in that he did not know of any religion other than those of the immediate Near East. He may have known something about Egyptian religion, and perhaps a little bit about Greek religion, but mostly he knew about Hebrew.

People who think that Jesus was God assume that he must have been omniscient. However, Saint Paul makes it perfectly clear in the Epistle to the Philippians that Jesus renounced his divine powers so as to be Man.

"Let this mind be in you which was also in Christ Jesus, who, being in the form of God, thought not equality with God a thing to be hung on to, but humbled himself and made himself of no reputation and was found in fashion as a man and became obedient to death." Theologians call that kinosis, which means self-emptying. So obviously, an omnipotent and omniscient man would not really be a man.

Even if you take the very orthodox Catholic doctrine of the nature of Christ, that he was both true God and true man, you must say that, for true God to be united with true man, true God has to make a voluntary renunciation, for the time being, of omniscience . . . and omnipotence and omnipresence, too, for that matter.

Now Jesus did say to his elect disciples, as recorded in John, "Before Abraham was, I am. I am the way, the truth, and the life. I am the resurrection and the life. I am the living bread that comes down from heaven. I and the Father are One, and who has seen me has seen the Father." There can be no mistaking that language. The Jews found out what he said and they put him to death, or had him put to death, for blasphemy. This is no cause for any special antagonism to the Jews, because it has always been done. It happened to one of the great Sufi mystics in Persia who had the same experience.

So, what happened? The apostles did not quite get the point. They were awed by the miracles of Jesus, and they worshiped him as people worship gurus, and you know to what lengths that can go. So the Christians said, "Okay, okay, Jesus of Nazareth was the Son of God. But let it stop right there! Nobody else!" So, Jesus was pedestalized. He was put in a position that was safely upstairs, so that his troubles and experience of cosmic consciousness would not come again and cause other people to be a nuisance. Those who had this experience, and expressed it during those times when the church had political power, were almost invariably persecuted. Giordano Bruno was burned at the stake. John Scotus Erigena was excommunicated. Meister Eckehart's theses were condemned, and so on and so on. A few mystics got away with it, but only because they used cautious language.

You see what happens. If you pedestalize Jesus you strangle the gospel at birth. *Gospel* means "good news," and I cannot for the life of me think what is the good news about the gospel as ordinarily handed down. Here is the revelation of God in Christ, in Jesus, and we are supposed to follow his life and example without having the advantage of being the boss's son. Now the tradition of both Catholic and Protestant fundamentalists represents Jesus to us as a freak, born of a virgin, knowing he is the Son of God, having the power of miracles, knowing that it is impossible to really kill him, because he is to rise again in the end. We do not know that about ourselves at all, but we are asked to take up our cross and follow him then. So what happens is this: We are delivered a gospel that is in fact an impossible religion. It is impossible to follow the way of Christ, and many a

Christian has admitted it. "I am a miserable sinner. I fall far short of the example of Christ." Christianity has institutionalized guilt as a virtue. Of course you will not come up to Jesus, ever, and therefore you will always be aware of your shortcomings. So, the more shortcomings you feel, the more you are aware of the vast abyss between Christ and yourself. You may go to confession, and if you have a nice, dear, understanding confessor, he will not get angry with you. Instead, he will say, "My child, you know you have sinned very grievously, but you must realize that the love of God and of our Lord is infinite, and that naturally you are forgiven. As a token of thanksgiving say three Hail Mary's." You may have committed a murder and robbed a bank and fornicated around and so on, and you feel awful about it—"I have wounded Jesus, grieved the Holy Spirit!"—but you also know in the back of your mind that you are going to do it all over again. You will not be able to help yourself. You will try and fail, and there will always be a greater and greater sense of guilt, and this is the Christianity of most people.

There is also a much more subtle Christianity of the theologians, the mystics, and the philosophers. It is not what gets preached from the pulpit, I grant you, by Billy Graham, and what I will call fundamentalist Catholics and Protestants. What would the real gospel be? The real good news is not simply that Jesus of Nazareth was the Son of God, but that he was a power-ful Son of God who came to open everybody's eyes to the fact that you too are a powerful son or daughter of God. This is perfectly plain if you go to the tenth chapter of John, verse thirty where Jesus says, "I and the Father are One." When he says that, there are some people around who are not intimate disciples, and they are hor-rified. They immediately pick up stones to stone him, and he says, "Many good works I have shown you from the Father, and for which of these do you stone me?" And they say, "For a good work we stone you not, but for blasphemy, because you, being a man, make yourself God." And he replied, quoting the eighty-second Psalm, "Is it not written in your law, 'I have said you are Gods?' If God called those to whom He gave His word Gods—and you cannot deny the scriptures—how can you say I blaspheme because I say I am a son of God?"

There is the whole thing in a nutshell. If you read the King James Bible—the version that descended with the angel—you will see that the words "Son of God," "the Son of God," "I am the Son of God," are in italics. Most people think the italics are for emphasis, but they are not. The italics indicate words interpolated by the translators, and you will not find that in the Greek. It says "a son of God." So here it seems to me perfectly plain that Jesus has it in the back of his mind that this is not something peculiar to himself when he says, "I am the way. No man comes to the Father but by me." This "I am," this "me," is the divine in us, which in Hebrew would be called the Lord, Adonai. A great deal is made of this by the esoteric Jews, the Cabalists and the Hasidim.

This knowledge has been perpetually repressed throughout the history of Western religion, because all Western religions have adopted the form of celestial monarchies and therefore have discouraged democracy in the kingdom of heaven. As a consequence of the teaching of the German and Flemish mystics in the fifteenth century, there began to be such movements as the Anabaptists, the Brothers of the Free Spirit, the Levelers, and the Quakers. These spiritual movements came to this country and helped to found a republic and not a monarchy. How could you say that a republic is the best form of government if you think that the universe is a monarchy? Obviously if God is on top in a monarchy, monarchy is the best form of government. Ever so many citizens of this republic think that they ought to believe that the universe is a monarchy, and therefore they are always at odds with the republic. It is principally from white, racist Christians that we have the threat of fascism in this country, because they have a religion that is militant, which is not the religion of Jesus. His religion was the realization of divine sonship, but the religion about Jesus pedestalizes him, and says that only this man, of all the sons of woman, was divine. It speaks of itself as the church militant. Onward Christian soldiers, marching as to war. It's utterly exclusive, convinced in advance of examining the doctrines of any other religion that it is the top religion. So it becomes a freak religion, just as it has made a freak of Jesus, by insisting he is an unnatural man.

It claims uniqueness, not realizing that what it teaches would be far more credible if it were truly Catholic, that is to say, universal, if it restated the truths that have been known from time immemorial, and have appeared in all the great cultures of the world. I suppose even very liberal Protestants still want to say "Yes, these other religions are very good. God has no doubt revealed Himself through Buddha and Lao-tzu, but they are not the top religion." Now, you can be loyal to Jesus, just as you are loyal to your own country, but you are not serving your country if you think that it is necessarily the best of all possible countries. That is doing a disservice to your country because it is refusing to be critical where criticism is proper. This is also true of religion. Every religion should be self-critical. Otherwise it soon degenerates into self-righteous hypocrisy. When we apply this proper criticism to the religion about Jesus we see that he was speaking not from a kind of weird, extraordinary, historical event, but with a voice that joins in saying what others have said before, in every place and time: "Wake up. Wake up and realize who you are."

I do not think that the church is going to have very much relevance until it gets with Jesus' actual teachings. Popular Protestantism and popular Catholicism are saying nothing about mystical religion, however. The message of the preacher, fifty-two Sundays a year, is "Dear people, be good." We have heard it ad nauseam. He may occasionally give a sermon on what happens after death, or on the nature of God, but basically the sermon is "Be good." But the real question is, How are we going to change for the good without a vital religious experience, and by this I refer to something much more profound than emoting over singing "Onward Christian Soldiers."

The problem with our ecclesiastical goings-on is that we run a talking shop. We pray, we tell God what to do or give Him advice, as if He did not know. We read the Scriptures. Jesus said, "You search the Scriptures daily, for in them you think you have life." Saint Paul made some rather funny references to "the spirit which giveth life and the letter which kills." I think the Bible ought to be ceremoniously and reverently burned every Easter, in faith that we need it no more because the spirit is with us. It is a dangerous book, and to worship it is of course a far more dangerous idolatry than bowing down to images of wood and stone. Nobody can reasonably confuse a wooden image with God, but you can very easily confuse a set of ideas with God, because concepts are more rarefied and abstract.

This endless talking and preaching in church does nothing, by and large, but excite a sense of anxiety and guilt. You cannot love out of that. No scolding or rational demonstration of the right way to behave is going to inspire people with love. Something else must happen. But you say, "Well, what are we going to do about it?" Do about it? Have you no faith? Then be quiet. But even Quakers are not quiet. They sit in meeting and think. However, suppose we are really quiet, and do not think, but are absolutely silent through and through. We tend to feel uncomfortable with this idea and say, "You will just fall into a blank space." But have you ever tried?

I feel then, that it is enormously important that churches stop being talking shops. They must become centers of contemplation. What is contemplation? It is what you do in the temple. You do not come to the temple to chatter but to be still and know that "I am God." This is why, if the Christian religion, if the gospel of Christ is to mean anything at all—instead of just being one of the forgotten religions, along with Mithraism— we must see Christ as the great mystic, in the proper sense of the word. A mystic is not someone who has all sorts of magical powers and understands spirits and so on. A mystic is one who realizes union with God. This seems to me the crux and message of the gospel. It is summed up in the prayer Saint John records Jesus speaking over his disciples: "May you be one, even as the Father and I are one, that you may be all one." May we all realize this divine sonship or daughtership or oneness, this basic identity with the eternal energy of the universe, the love that moves the sun and other stars.

DEMOCRACY IN THE KINGDOM OF HEAVEN

CHAPTER FOUR

T he great discussion going on in what we call the new theology is the revolution within standard-brand Christianity. For years and years the clergy—the ministry of the various churches such as Episcopalian, Methodist, Baptist, Congregational, Unitarian, even in some cases Disciples of Christ and Lutheran—have been discussing religion in their theological seminaries in terms utterly different from what you normally hear from the pulpit. Every graduate of an intelligent theological school has a sense of intense frustration as they go out to work in a community or parish church. This is because they do not believe in what they are supposed to preach. And this has, in a way, been true for a long, long time.

Clergy, except in the Roman Catholic Church where the situation is somewhat different, are very heavily controlled by the laity because he who pays the piper calls the tune. Therefore they are in a state of constant frustration because those who contribute most heavily, and therefore are most interested in the church, tend to be conservative people. They want that old-time religion, although as a matter of fact, what they call the old-time religion is really quite modern. But that is what they want.

In the British army they have a thing called church parade. There is a famous story about a drill sergeant who would get all the troops up for church parade on a Sunday morning, and then he would call out, "Catholics to the right, Protestants to the left, fancy religions in the middle." To the degree that intelligent people in our culture have any religion at all, it tends to be a fancy religion, one of the new kinds such as Unity, Christian Science, Theosophy, Buddhism, Vedanta, or some kind of special Protestant offshoot such as the Fellowship Church in San Francisco or the Community Church in New York, that are very liberal, very left-wing theologically.

The new theology has emerged at this time because to a very large extent, the clergy are fed up. Christianity has its back to the wall, and the Pope knows this better than anybody. So hand in hand with this ecumenical movement there comes a reconsideration of what on earth Christianity is all about. Is there *one* God? Is there a God at all? A lot of people are boldly saying all ideas of God are to be abandoned.

As an English priest by the name of Father Mascal put it, the basic assumption of the secularist movement in Christian theology is that life is a journey between the maternity ward and the crematorium. That is all there is; that's it. That is the only life the Christian religion has to encounter. Therefore, with this abandonment of God, and even the idea that the universe is supernaturally controlled, the Christian religion fastens itself with peculiar and increased fervor to the figure of Jesus of Nazareth. As one wit put it, there is no God, and Jesus Christ is His only son.

There is something strange about Christianity. It shares with Islam and Judaism what we might call theological imperialism. Christians of even the most liberal stripe fervently believe that their religion is the best religion. They say, "Jesus Christ is the only Son of God." That isn't really an orthodox way of saying it, but it is the way orthodox people do say it. Otherwise they say, "Jesus is the greatest man who ever lived." The point is that you make a commitment to the following of Jesus as an historical personage. And for some reason or other, people who commit themselves to this exclusive kind of following of Jesus become exceedingly obstreperous. They will either damn other religions outright or, far more insidious, damn them with faint praise. "Old Buddha taught some very good things, and we all are indebted to his great moral principles." But there always follows a pitch for the sole following of Jesus as the Lord and Master, head and shoulders above all.

The trouble with that has always been that when you get into a theological argument with a person who is this kind of Christian, you find yourself in a situation where the advocate and the judge are the same person. That is to say, Jesus is found to be the best man in the world by the standards of Christianity, because those are the standards with which this kind of person judges. Therefore, you will find that people who leap to these judgments usually do not know very much about any other kind of religion. The courses on comparative religion in theological schools are shockingly superficial and grossly inaccurate. This is coming to the front now. The real purpose of belonging to the church is to be saved, and being saved means belonging to the most "in" group. You have to be part of a select group if you want to know who you are, to distinguish yourself, because then you know you are different from the people who are not part of your group. There you get a contrast. This is the basic arrangement for a church. If you want to be in some kind of an insider's group, you must put everybody else beyond the pale.

Saint Thomas Aquinas actually gave the show away when he said that the blessed in heaven will often walk to the battlements and look down and delight in the justice of God being properly carried out in hell. But you may be very liberal, you may not believe in hell. After all, it is not nice or sophisticated nowadays to believe in everlasting damnation. So we have new phrases for it, such as "failing to be a real person," "sinking below the human level," or "entering into final and irremediable psychosis." All of these are new phrases for either damnation or heresy. So you can know you are saved only if you know that somebody else is not. It is very difficult to imagine a state of affairs wherein everyone and everything is saved. You have to be a mystic even to think about that, because it requires a state of consciousness that transcends oppositions, and you cannot do that with ordinary logic. You have to have a new kind of logic, the kind I am using at the moment when I point out that damned people and saved people need each other. They are in a symbiotic relationship. They go together in the same way as the back and front of something do, because if something has a front it has to have a back too. And so the very fact that fronts and backs go together indicates that there is a unity between opposites, even such apparent opposites as the damned and the saved.

It is only as you begin to realize you need the damned people in order to be saved, and they need the saved in order to be damned, that you can start laughing about it. And of course that laughter is very subversive. You know the rules: you are not supposed to laugh in church, or in courts of law, either. They are places where laughter makes people nervous, because laughter is supposed to be a sign of disrespect. However, that may not be so at all. Dante said that the song of the angels in paradise sounded like the laughter of the universe. But in church—especially in the more serious kind—laughing is very bad form. Why? Because if you look at the design of a Catholic Church you will notice it is based on the design of the courtroom of a king. If you look at a Protestant church you will see that it is based upon the design of a law court. Indeed, the Protestant minister wears exactly the same robes as an American judge, and all those pews and boxlike stalls are the same as you will find in the old-fashioned court with the witness box and jury box. This is the original idea of the Christian church.

An ancient Roman church is called a basilica. That means the courtroom of a king, or the throne room. The altar is the throne of God, but in a courtroom the king is very nervous, because anybody who takes it on himself to govern other people and rule must always watch out. Therefore he always has his back to the wall, and he is flanked by attending guards and high ministers of state. Just so that nobody will get up and make trouble, he has them either on their knees or flat on their faces when they are in his presence. And, of course, no one must laugh. That would be laughing at Mr. Big.

This was the pattern or the model on which the Judeo-Christian idea of God was based, and it is a political model. The titles for God—King of Kings, Lord of

Lords—were taken from those of the supreme emperors of Persia. So at morning prayer in the English church the clergyman gets up and says, "Almighty and everlasting God, the only ruler of princes, King of Kings, Lord of Lords, who dost from thy throne behold all dwellers on earth, most graciously deign to behold our gracious sovereign lady Queen Elizabeth and all the royal family." You may not believe literally that God sits on a throne, or even has a body to put on one, or that He wears a crown, or that He has a beard, but that image still colors your feeling about the character of God. Images are more powerful than intellectual concepts.

You may know that it says in the prayer book that God is a spirit without a body or passions, omnipresent to all places, and eternal to all time. Therefore one thinks, as Hegel does, of the gaseous vertebrate, or else of an enormously diffused sea of luminous Jell-O filling all time and space. Everybody uses images. But behind those images are the old images that influenced us in childhood. If you still attend church and use that imagery, emotionally you still feel toward God as you would if you took it literally. This political model of God has dominated the West. The world is related to God as subjects are to a king, or as artifacts are to their maker. We have a ceramic model of the universe, because it is said in the Book of Genesis that God made Adam out of the dust of the ground. In other words, He made a clay figure and blew the breath of life into the nostrils of the figurine and it came to life.

The Hindus do not have to cope with this model of the universe because they do not see the universe as God's creation—in the sense of being an artifact—they see it as God's drama. They see the world as active, not created. God is that which is pretending to be all that is. Everybody is really God, a mask of God, who is playing that He is you. But he is doing it so well that He has taken himself in. He is both the audience and the actor. He wants to get you crying. He wants to get you sitting on the edge of your seat in anticipation. God, the ultimate actor, has convinced Himself completely that the act is real.

The Chinese have a third model. Theirs is of an organic universe, a great organism. It is alive; it grows. It is an intelligent order.

Those are the three great models of the world. When, a long time ago, the West stopped believing seriously in God, we Westerners still retained the idea of the world as an artifact, we merely graduated from a ceramic model of the universe to a fully automatic, mechanical model, which is now common sense for most people living today.

I return to the point that the clergy and people of the church do not really believe at all in God in the old-fashioned sense of the word. If they did seriously believe the Christian religion in its orthodox form, they would be screaming in the street. But even the Jehovah's Witnesses are more or less polite when they come and call at your house. If they really believed that you were going to hell, they would make a bigger fuss about you than they would if you had the bubonic plague. But nobody really takes Christianity that seriously anymore, because they do not believe in it. They know they ought to believe in it. In fact many sermons are exhortations to have more faith, which means that we all recognize that we do not really believe it, but we ought to. We feel very guilty about it, but we do not have the moral strength to believe in this. However, it is not only a matter of moral strength. It is a matter of being asked to believe in something that most people feel is nonsense, which is that the world is run on the lines of a state. How can you be a citizen of the United States, having taken an oath that a republican form of government is the best form of government, and believe that the universe is a monarchy?

Intelligent people have always realized that this political model for the cosmos will not do. Actually, no serious theologian ever did believe that God was an old gentleman with whiskers sitting on a golden throne. Never. The bishop of Woolidge says in his book *Honest To God* that there is not that sort of a someone out there. He is very naive in a way. He could have taken huge quotations out of Saint Thomas Aquinas, out of the great fathers of the church, from Origen, from Clement of Alexandria, from Saint Gregory Nazianzen, from Saint John of Damascus, from Saint Basil the Great, from Saint Augustine, from Saint Ambrose, from Bernard of Clairvaux, and Albert the Great; he could have quoted all those perfectly orthodox, very correct theologians and shown that they never believed in a God with whiskers. He could have come forward and said, "See, this is a perfectly orthodox book, and I am not a revolutionary. I am just going back to the real old-time religion." He did not do that, and do you know why? He told me. He had never read those writers in theological school. His religious training was entirely confined to biblical studies, and never got that far.

It is the same with ever so many people. One of the reasons so many people turn to an Oriental religion is that the intellectual level at which Oriental religions were first presented in the West was so much higher than the intellectual level at which Christianity was presented in the local church. If you lived in India, or Ceylon, of course you would attend the local Buddhist monastery, and its sermons would be just as junky as the stuff taught at our local churches. They do not tell people about things like the great void, or how to practice meditation—

that is for specialists. All they care about is gaining merit, earning better circumstances in your next life, or getting out of evil karma. That is what popular Buddhism really is about. The trouble in the West is that everybody is becoming educated, and there is a terrific degree of literacy. Therefore the public has to be treated with respect. You cannot say "the public be damned" anymore. There are too many educated people.

I would say the God that really is dead is this politically modeled God, however conceived. The divine paternalistic authority who rules the universe—to whom you as an ego are related, by analogy, as a subject is to a king—is just not holding up. But what are the alternatives for Western people with a Christian background? What other kind of God could we have? One of the possibilities is no God at all. This is what people on the far left of this new theology are saying. A man like James Pike, on the other hand, is on the new theology's right wing. He very definitely believes in God—he is a theist—but he does not believe in anything with whiskers on it, nor does he really believe in the political model.

We must choose, then, between a mechanical universe that is no more than it appears to be, and a very refined conception of a God that would be called "It" instead of "He." It makes a very powerful difference which pronoun you use. Even "He-She," as the Christian Scientists talk about the "father-mother," is sort of complicated. "It" is rather simple. But then when you say "it," does this mean that God is like electricity that does not seem to have any independent intelligence of its own, but is just energy, something that goes "zoom?" Is God, as an "it," something like that?

The funny thing is it is very difficult to be a real atheist. In 1928 in the House of Parliament in England, the Church of England wanted a new revised prayer book. However, because the church and the state are inseparable in England, the houses of Parliament had to vote on whether the new prayer book might be used. Somebody got up and said, "It is perfectly ridiculous that an assemblage which contains a number of atheists should vote on the inner politics of the Church of England." But another member got up and said, "I don't think there are any atheists here, not really. We all believe in some sort of a something somewhere."

Now in the theological world, it just doesn't do to believe in "some sort of a something somewhere," because one thing that theologians detest is vagueness. Even no God at all is preferred to vagueness, because at least atheism is clear and precise. You should hear what they say. "No beating around the bush old man. You know it is just fuzzy thinking to believe in a great universal mind that is an undifferentiated aesthetic continuum, and that is all there is to 'some sort of a something somewhere.' This is woolly thinking. Either give us no God, or else give us a God with a definite character and a clear moral will and precise standards who will not be pushed around, a God with biblical quality."

What do you do? Do you separate your mind into two different compartments, in one of which you keep abreast of science and the modern world, while in the other you simply have nothing to do with all that? To combine those two compartments would make very difficult the possibility of belief in the ludicrous propositions that are usually called religion. But a lot of people want a religion that is difficult to believe in because they feel that difficult beliefs are a kind of a test of faith.

So there is a possibility of that kind of God, and there is also the possibility of no God. Is life just this trip from the maternity ward to the crematorium, and is the purpose of religion just the improvement of that trip?

That is to say, is the whole business of religion to get rid of poverty and war and exploitation and disease, or is there something else? Those who take the view that there is nothing else, which we will call the secular position in theology, are of course strongly influenced by contemporary philosophy—especially in that form that is called scientific empiricism or logical positivism—which maintains that the idea of God is not a fallacy, but is a meaningless idea. In other words, they maintain that the propositions that God exists, and that God is the origin and creator and governor of everything that is happening are utterly devoid of meaning. It is to them as if one were to say "Everything is up." They maintain that no logical proposition whatsoever can be made about all propositions because all propositions are labels on boxes and you cannot have the box containing all boxes, because this box would have no outside, and therefore it would not be a box. All propositions, all words, must refer to classes of some kind, and you cannot have the class of all classes.

Secularists also say that the notion of a God is meaningless on the grounds that it does not help you to make any predictions. Or they ask, What evidence would completely satisfy you as disproving the existence of God? And no believer in God can think of any evidence that would conclusively prove that there isn't a God. Similarly, psychoanalysts are completely incapable of thinking of any evidence that would disprove the existence of the Oedipus complex. So on logical grounds contemporary philosophers take the position that the idea of God is a meaningless idea. And since many theologians are influenced by modern philosophy, they take these arguments seriously and would like to secularize the whole conception of religion or, to put it in Bonhoeffer's words, "Have Christianity without religion."

When I hear someone say that there is nothing to life except the trip between the maternity ward and the crematorium, I recall having heard something like that before. When asked, "What is the Buddha?" a Chinese master replied, "It's windy again this morning." Another Buddhist master, on his deathbed, wrote the poem, "From the bathtub to the bathtub I have uttered stuff and nonsense." This is the bathtub in which the baby is washed at birth and the bathtub in which the corpse is washed before burial. "All the time between," he said, "I was going yakety-yak." Now, do those poems mean what they say? Not quite. They are based on a life devoted to the discipline of a very particular kind of meditation that culminates in a completely shattering experience, which is very difficult to talk about. Generally speaking, it is the encounter with eternity, with the eternal—not necessarily in the sense of that which goes on and on through time, but the eternal as the timeless that transcends time and is beyond measurement in terms of hours and days. When a person who is in that state of consciousness, or has been through it, looks at the ordinary, everyday world, he sees the ordinary, everyday world as we see it, but with a very extraordinary difference. If we have to put that difference into some sort of Western, Christian-influenced language, he would perhaps say, "Don't you realize that sitting around here in this room, with our ordinary, everyday faces and clothes and personalities, we are sitting smack in the middle of the beatific vision? This sitting here in this room is precisely infinity and eternity. It is it. This is the beatific vision. This is God."

In this meditation religion, they still have temples, they still have buddhas, and they still chant sutras and offer incense and ring gongs and all that kind of thing, but they also say that to really get to the highest level of religion you have to kill the Buddha.

Supposing a clergyman got up one day in the pulpit and said, "Every time you say Jesus Christ, you have to wash out your mouth." Or, "If you meet God the Father, kill Him. If you meet God the Son, kill Him. If you meet God the Holy Spirit, kill It. If you meet Saint Augustine, kill him. Kill them all right away." This is simply translating into Christian terms what a Buddhist teacher said in about the year 800 A.D.

However, I do not think this "killing Buddha" is what is happening in the new theology. I think they are just getting rid of God.

We are supposed to believe in the Ten Commandments, and one of them says, "Thou shalt not make to thyself any graven image of anything that is in heaven above, or the earth beneath, nor bow down, nor worship them." What I have been talking about—this killing of Buddha—is a destruction of idols, because the most dangerous graven images are not those that are made of wood and stone, they are those that are made of ideas. It is well known to the great mystical traditions all over the world that the supreme vision can only come when you have rid your mind of every idea of God whatsoever. It would be like cleaning a window on which somebody has painted blue sky. To see the true sky you have got to scrape off the paint. You may say, "My goodness, you shouldn't take that nice blue painting off. It was done by a great artist. See how pretty the clouds are. You mustn't do that because we won't have any of the blue sky anymore." But the great mystics have always ceased to cling to God, because the only God you can cling to is the idea of God.

In order to discover God you have to stop clinging entirely. Why does one cling to God? For safety, of course. You want to save something; you want to save yourself. I don't care what you mean by saved, whether it means just feeling happy, or that life is meaningful, or that there is somebody up there who cares. If you do not cling to one god, you cling to another: the state, money, sex, yourself, power. These are all false gods. But there has to come a time when clinging stops; only then does the time of faith begin. People who hold on to God do not have any faith at all, because real faith lies in not holding on to anything.

In the Christian tradition this nonclinging is called the cloud of unknowing. There is a book about it written by a fourteenth-century British monk. He got it from a man called Dionysius the Areopagite, who had assumed the name of Saint Paul's Athenian convert, a Syrian monk living in the sixth century. Meister Eckehart, Saint Thomas Aquinas, John Scotus Erigena, and many other great medieval theologians studied Dionysius the Areopagite. His book was *The Theologica Mystica,* in which he explained that, in order to come to full union with God, you must give up every conception of God whatsoever. And he enumerates the concepts that must be given up: don't think that God is a oneness or a threeness or a unity or a spirit or any kind of anything that the human mind can conceive. He is beyond all that.

This is called apophatic theology, a Greek term that contrasts with catophatic. When you speak catophatically you say what God is like. Dionysius also wrote a book of catophatic theology called *The Divine Names.* Catophatic theology tells what God is like according to analogy. He is like a father. We do not say God is a cosmic male parent but that he is, in some respect, like a father. This is the catophatic method. The apophatic method says what God is not. All those theologians who followed Dionysius said that the highest way of talking about God is in negative terms, just as, to use Dionysius's own image, when a sculptor makes a figure he does it entirely by removing stone, by taking away. In that same spirit, Saint Thomas Aquinas said, "Because God, by His infinity, exceeds every idea to which the human mind can reach, the best way to speak of Him is by removal." That is, removing from our view of God every inadequate concept. This what the Hindus refer to as *neti neti,* saying of the Brahman of the supreme reality, "It is not this, it is not this."

This intellectual operation of destroying concepts must go hand in hand with the psychological operation of ceasing to cling to any image whatsoever. Simply cease to cling, because there is no need to. There is no need to cling because when you were born you were kicked off a precipice. There was a big explosion, and you are falling, and a lot of other things are falling with you, including some pretty large lumps of rock, of which one is called the earth. It will not help you to cling to the rocks, when they are falling, too. It may give you an illusion of safety, but everything is falling, and falling apart. The ancients said, in the words of Heraclitus, "All is transient, all flows." You cannot cling to anything; it is like grabbing at smoke with a nonexistent hand. Clinging only makes people anxious.

When you come to the realization that you cannot cling to anything, that there is nothing to cling to, there transpires a change of consciousness that we can call either faith or letting go. In Sanskrit they put it this way: *tat tvam asi,* meaning literally "That are thou," or as we would say, "You are it." And if you are God, then you cannot have an idea of God any more than you can chew your own teeth. You do not need any idea of God. The sun does not need to shine on itself. Knives do not need to cut themselves. All the things you see on the outside are states of the nervous system in the brain. When the Zen master suddenly discovered that carrying a pail with water in it was a miracle, he realized there isn't anything except God. If you really know that, you don't need to have a religion. You can have one, because it is a free world, but you don't need one. All religion—any outward manifestation of religion—is pure gravy after that realization. It is like a man with lots of money making some more; it is quite unnecessary.

According to the very best theologians, it was never necessary for God to create the world; it did not add anything to Him. He did not have to do it, was under no compulsion. He did it out of what Dionysius the Areopagite called—to anglicize it—super fullness, or, in other words, for kicks. We do not like using that kind of language in connection with God, but it is completely contemporary and exactly right. That is what the Bible says, only it puts it in a more sedate way. It says, "His majesty did it for his pleasure." That is the way you talk about somebody who is the king. As Queen Victoria said, "We are not amused."

It says in the Book of Proverbs that the divine wisdom speaks as an attribute of God, but standing aside from God, in a sort of primitive polytheism. The goddess Wisdom says that in the beginning of the world her delight was to play before the divine presence, and especially to play with the sons of men. The word in Hebrew is "play," but in the King James translation it is "rejoice," because that is a more sedate word. You may rejoice in church, but not play. You may not have fun in church, but you may rejoice. Do you see the difference? The point of the matter is that there was no reason to make the world, and it was done just to make celestial whoopee. Alleluia. That is why the angels are laughing. Only when you hear it in church, everybody has forgotten what *alleluia* means. Alleluia is like bird's song. Bird song is not about anything, it is just for kicks. Why do you sing? Why do you like dancing? What is music for? For kicks. That is what alleluia is. When nothing is being clung to, one gets to the point where everything blows up. That is what is meant in Zen by satori, "sudden awakening." You suddenly see, "Good heavens, what was I making all that fuss about?" Because here we are. This, right here, is what we have been looking for all the time. It was right here.

Many little children know from the beginning what life is all about, only they haven't got the words to tell us. That is the whole problem with child psychology. What child psychologists are looking for ideally is an articulate baby who can explain what it is like to be a baby, but they will never find one. By the time you teach a child to speak, you mess it up. You give it language, but it can't think big thoughts with this funny, limited language, especially using the words children are started out with. Then finally, when they've got the poor child completely hypnotized, they tell it the most preposterous things. They tell it that it must be free. They say, "You, child, are an independent agent, and you are responsible. Therefore we command you to love us. We require that you do something which will please us, and that you do it voluntarily." And no wonder people are mixed up!

I am afraid the new theology really is serious about there not being any God. The universe is therefore in rather a pitiful predicament. This is a continuation of the nineteenth century's philosophy of the fully automatic model, in which the universe is seen as essentially stupid, a mechanism, a gyration of blind energy in which human beings and human intelligence and values are flukes, and rather uncomfortable ones, because nature does not give a damn about us. And because it doesn't, we have got to fight it.

All of that is pure mythology. It is grossly unscientific, but most people believe it. It is common sense, today. But what an opportunity there is in the new theology, and in the whole ferment now going on, to get people to see another point of view, and realize that when you get rid of God, all you are doing is destroying an idol. All idols must be respectfully destroyed, but not the way those wretched Puritans went around destroying all the figures of saints in the stained glass windows in the medieval churches. That was a disrespectful iconoclasm. An example of respectful iconoclasm would be the ceremonial burning of the Bible every Easter Sunday, because if Jesus is truly risen from the dead, you do not need the Bible anymore, you do not need any books. Burn it ceremoniously, and with great respect, but not with too much seriousness, because certainly God does not take Himself seriously. If He did, I should not like to think what would happen.

THE IMAGES OF MAN

CHAPTER FIVE

I want to start by giving what may be a new defini-
tion of myth. Normally *myth* means tale, a fable, a
falsehood, or an idea that is out of date, something
untrue. But another older, stricter use of the word
means not something untrue, but rather an image in
terms of which people make sense of life and the world.
For example, suppose you do not understand the techni-
calities of electricity, and somebody wanted to explain
about the flow of currents. He might compare electricity
to water, and because you understand water, you may
get some idea about the behavior of electricity. An
astronomer explaining what he means by expanding
space will use the metaphor of a balloon, a black balloon

with white spots on it. The white spots represent the galaxies, and if you blow up the balloon, they all get farther away from each other at the same speed as the balloon blows up. We are not saying that electricity is water, or that the universe is the balloon with white spots on it, but that they are something like that.

In the same way, the human being has always used images to represent his deepest ideas of the working of the universe, and man's place in it. I am going to discuss certain aspects of two of the greatest myths, in this sense of the word, that have influenced mankind's thinking. First is the myth of the universe as an artifact, something made as a carpenter makes tables, chairs, houses, or as a potter makes pots, or a sculptor makes figurines. The other is the image of the world as a drama, in which all the things in the world are not made, but acted, in the same way as a player acts parts. These are the two great images that govern respectively the religions of the West descended from Hebraism—Hebraism itself, Christianity, Islam—and the religions of the East, with their origin in India: Hinduism in particular, and to a lesser extent, Buddhism.

I want to make it perfectly plain, before I go any further, that in talking about these two great religious traditions in terms of images, I am talking about the way they express themselves at a rather popular level. Sophisticated Christians and Hindus think beyond images. For example, a Christian may think of God as the father, but a sophisticated and educated Christian does not imagine that God is a cosmic male parent with a white beard sitting on a golden throne above the stars. Nor does a Hindu imagine literally that God is the super showman, the big actor. These images are what it is like, not what it is, and perhaps when I get through with discussing them we will be able to ask whether any of these images still make sense to us in this twentieth century, when we have a view of the world so powerfully shaped by Western science.

I begin with a few aspects of the image of the world, and thus the image of man, as it comes to us from the Hebrew Bible. It says in the Book of Genesis that the Lord God created man out of the dust of the earth, as if He had made a clay figure of Adam. He blew the breath of life into its nostrils and the figurine became alive. It says that the figurine was made in the image of God. God, who is conceived in this particular image as a personal, living, intelligent spirit, creates in man something similar. This is very definitely a creation, as the potter makes a pot out of clay. For the creature that the Lord God has made is not God. The creature is something less than God, something like God but not God.

Some very interesting consequences follow from this idea of the world as an artifact. What follows is that the whole universe is seen as a marvelous technological accomplishment. If it was created, there must be an explanation of how it was made, and the whole history of Western thought has in many ways been an attempt to discover how the creator did it. What were the principles; what laws were laid down; what is the blueprint that underlies this creation? This image has persisted throughout Western history, and continues on into a time when very many people do not believe in Christianity, or Judaism, or Islam. They are agnostics or atheists, but they still carry with them something of this idea of the world as an artifact. If you are a Christian or a Jew, you believe that the world is an artifact of creation of the intelligent spirit called God. But if you are an atheist or an agnostic in this culture, you believe that the world is an automatic machine without a creator, something that made itself.

We might say that our original model of the universe was the ceramic model. The Bible is full of references to God as the potter who makes the world out of obedient clay. And even when Western thinkers in the eighteenth century began to drop the idea of a personal God, they still kept the idea of the artifact. So we could say that after the ceramic model of the universe, we got the fully automatic model.

Underlying our way of thinking about things is the question, How are they put together? And if you want to find out, one of the obvious ways to proceed is to take them to pieces. Everybody knows that if you want to find out how something is made, you unscrew the parts and see what the secret is inside the box. So Western science in its beginnings took everything apart. It took animals apart; it took flowers apart; it took rocks apart.

When they got everything reduced to its tiniest pieces, they tried to find methods for taking those apart, too, so that we could eventually discover what the very smallest things were, and learn what method the creator, or the fully automatic universe, used in putting everything together. It was hoped that this would lead us to an understanding of how life works. Man himself was also looked on as a creation, as something that had been made. But there were some difficulties with this idea, because if you believe in the world in accordance with the fully automatic model, you really have got to admit that man, too, must be fully automatic, a machine rather than a person. Man, then, doffs his hat and says, "How do you do? I am a person. I am alive. I am sensible. I talk, I have feelings." But you wonder, "Does he really, or is he just an automaton?"

Under the dispensation of the fully automatic model, the Western image of man is that we are very sensitive, living beings, and that inside the human skin, by an extraordinary fluke of nature, there has arisen something called reason. There have also arisen "values," such as love. But these were flukes because they happened inside a fully automatic universe that, because it is merely automatic, must be stupid. In other words, you won't find anything really intelligent outside human skins. Therefore, the only thing that people can do if they want to maintain reason and love in this universe is to fight nature, and beat the stupid, external world into submission to the human will. So the war against nature is the great project of Western technology thus far, because each one of us has inherited from thousands of years of history a view of man as something made of breath breathed into a pot of clay. Each one feels himself to be a globule of consciousness or mind living inside a vehicle called "my body." Since the world outside that body is stupid, we feel estranged from the world.

When we find out how enormous the universe is, that makes us feel extremely unimportant and rather lonely, because our basic image of ourselves is of a soul, an ego, a mind by itself in its little house, looking out at a world that is strange, and saying, "That is not me." I am therefore a brief interval of consciousness between the darkness and the darkness. That is not too happy a thought. I would like to be able to believe that there is more to life than that. Many of us say, "If only I could believe that there is an intelligent and eternal God in whose eyes I am important, and who has the power to enable me to live forever, that would be very nice." But for many people that is an extraordinarily difficult thing to believe.

I want to contrast this ceramic image of the world with the distinctly different dramatic image, which is the presiding image of the Hindus. Their idea is that God did not make the world, but acted it. That is to say, every person and every thing is a role or part that the Godhead is playing. Of course, the Hindu image of God is a little bit different from the Jewish, the Christian, and the Islamic image. When I was a little boy, I used to ask my mother interminable questions. When she got sick of it, she said, "My dear, there are some things in life that we are just not meant to know." And I said, "Will we ever know?" And she said, "Yes, if you die and then go to heaven, God will explain it all."

I used to hope that on rainy afternoons in heaven we would all sit around the throne of grace and ask the Lord, "Why did you do this?" and "Why did you do that?" And He would explain.

Every child in the West asks his mother, "How was I made?" No person knows, but we think that perhaps God knows, and He will be able to explain. Likewise, if anybody becomes mentally deranged and claims to be God, we always humor such people by asking them technical questions, "How did you make the world in six days?" or, "If you are God, why couldn't you change this plate into a rabbit?" We do this because, in our popular image of God, God is the supreme technocrat. He knows all the answers. He understands everything in detail and can tell you all about it.

The Hindus don't think of God that way. If you ask the Hindu God, "How did you create the human body?" He would say, "I know how I did it, but it can't be explained in words because words are too clumsy. In words I have to talk about things slowly. I have to string them out, because words run in a line, and lines add up to books, and books add up to libraries. If I explain to you how I made the human organism, it will take all eternity. I don't have to understand things in words in order to make them happen. Nor do you." You don't have to understand in words how to breathe. You just breathe. You don't have to understand in words how to grow your hair, how to shape your bones, how to make your eyes blue or brown, you just do it. And somebody who does understand to some extent—a physiologist, perhaps—can't do it any better than you.

That is the Hindu idea of divine omnipotence, and that is why their images of the gods very often have many arms. You will often see the god Shiva with ten arms, or the Buddhist Avalokiteshvara with one thousand arms. Their image of the divine is of a sort of centipede. A centipede can move a hundred legs without having to think about it, and Shiva can move ten arms very dexterously without having to think about them. You know what happened to the centipede when it stopped to think how to move a hundred legs; it got all balled up. So the Hindus do not think of God as being a technician in the sense of having a verbal or mathematical understanding of how the world is created. It is just done simply, like that. If we had to describe this simple way in words it would be very complicated, but God, in the Hindus' idea, does not need to do so.

The Hindu does not see any fundamental division between God and the world. The world is God at play; the world is God acting. How did they arrive at such an idea? Very simply. When you try to think about why there is a world at all, you realize it is extraordinarily odd that there should be anything. It would have been much simpler and would have required a great deal less energy for there to have been nothing. But here everything is. Why? Well, what would you do if you were God? Suppose that every night you could dream any dream you wanted. What would you dream? I am quite sure that most of us would dream of all the marvelous things we wanted to have happen to us. We would fulfill all our wishes. We might go on that way for months, and we could make it extraordinarily rich by dreaming seventy-five years full of glorious happenings in one night.

After you had done that for a few months, though, you might begin to get a little tired of it and say, "What about an adventure tonight, in which something terribly exciting and rather dangerous is going to happen? But I will know I am dreaming so it won't be too bad, and I'll wake up if it gets too serious." So you do that for a while; you rescue princesses from dragons, and all sorts of things. Then after doing that for some time, you might say, "Let's go a bit further. Let's forget it's a dream, and have a real thrill." Ooh! But you know you will wake up. Then, after you have done that for a while, you will dare yourself to get out as far as you can, and you will end up dreaming the life you are living right now.

The reason for this, the Hindu would say, is that the basic pulse of life, the basic motivation of existence, is like the game of hide-and-seek. Now you see it, now you don't. Everything is based on that; all life is vibration, pulsation. Light is a pulsation of light and dark. Sound is a pulsation of sound and silence. Everything is going back and forth at various speeds. The motion of a wave consists of two pulses, the crest and the trough. You can't have crests without troughs; you can't have troughs without crests. They always go together. You can't have hide without seek; you can't have seek without hide. You can't have here without there; if you didn't know where there was, you wouldn't know where here was. You can't have is without isn't, because you don't know what you mean by is unless you also know what you mean by isn't, and vice versa.

Hide-and-seek is the fundamental game of the universe, in the Hindu view. It is as if the Lord God, or

Brahman, had said in the beginning, "Get lost, man. Disappear. I'll find you again later." When the disappearance gets very far out, the contrary rhythm begins, the dreamer wakes up and says, "Whoo, that's a relief." Then after a period of rest, in which everything is at peace, it starts all over again. The spirit of adventure springs eternal.

The Hindus, for their period in history, had extremely vast ideas of space and time. They had the theory that the hiding part of the universal game goes on for 4,320,000 years; a period called a *kalpa* in Sanskrit. The "dreaming" part is followed by the "waking" part. The dreaming is the hiding where the Godhead imagines that it is all of us. Then for another 4,320,000 years there is a period of awakening, and at the end of that begins the dream again. The dreaming period is further subdivided into four stages. The first stage is the longest, and it is the best. During that stage, the dream is beautiful. The second stage is not quite so long, and is a little unsettling. There is an element of instability in it, a certain touch of insecurity. In the third stage, which is shorter still, the forces of light and the forces of darkness—or good and evil—are equally balanced, and things are beginning to look rather dangerous. In the fourth stage, the shortest of them all, the negative, dark, or evil side triumphs, and the whole thing blows up in the end. But that is like the bang in a dream when you get shot, and you wake up, and see it was just a dream after all. There is a waking period, and then the whole thing starts again.

You will notice, if you make the computation, that in this drama the forces of the dark side are operative for one-third of the time; the forces of the light side for two-thirds of the time. This is a very ingenious arrangement; we see in it the fundamental principles of drama.

Suppose this is not a lecture tonight but a show. There are actors coming on the stage, but they are real people like you. In order for you not to see them in that way, they are going to put on their costumes and makeup, and then they are going to come out in front here and pretend to various roles. And you know you want to be half convinced that what they are doing on the stage is real. The work of a great actor is to get you sitting on the edge of your chair, anxious, or weeping, or roaring with laughter, because he has almost persuaded you that what is on the stage is really happening. That is the greatness of his art, to take the audience in.

In the same way, the Hindu feels that the Godhead acts his part so well that he takes himself in completely. And each one of you is the godhead, wonderfully fooled by your own act. And although you won't admit it to yourself, you are enjoying it like anything.

When you say "I am a person," the word *person* is from the drama. When you open a play script and see the list of the actors, this is the dramatis personae, the persons of the drama. The word *person* in Latin is *persona,* meaning "through sound," or something through which sound comes; the persona in Greek or Roman drama was the mask worn by the actors. And because they acted on an open-air stage, the mask's mouth was shaped like a small megaphone that would project the sound. So the person is the mask. Isn't it funny how we have forgotten that? Harry Emerson Fosdick could write a book called *On Being a Real Person*, which translated literally is, "How to be a genuine fake," because in the old sense, the person is the role, the part played by the actor. But if you forget that you are the actor, and think you are the person, you have been taken in by your own role. You are "en-rolled," or bewitched, spellbound, enchanted.

Something else about the nature of drama is that there must be a villain, unless of course you are acting some kind of a nonplay that does not have any story. Fundamentally, all stories start out with the status quo. Everybody is just sort of going along, and then some problem comes in to upset everything. The interest of the play lies in the question, How are we going to solve that problem? It is the same when you play cards. If you are playing solitaire, you start by shuffling the deck, introducing chaos. The game is to play order against chaos. In the drama there must be a villain, a dark side, so that the hero can play against him, and it. If you go to the theater for a good cry, then you let the villain win and you call it a tragedy. If you go for a thrill, you let the hero win. If you go for laughs, you call it a comedy. There can be various arrangements between the hero and the villain, but when the curtain goes down at the end of the drama, the hero and the villain always step out hand in hand and the audience applauds both. They do not boo the villain at the end of the play. They applaud him for acting the part of the villain so well, and they applaud the hero for acting the part of the hero so well, because they know that the hero and the villain are only roles, masks.

Behind the stage is the green room. After the play is over, and before it begins, the masks are there. The Hindus feel that behind the scene, under the surface of reality, you are all actors, marvelously skilled at playing parts and in getting lost in the mazes of your own minds and the entanglements of your own affairs, as if this were the most urgent thing going on. But behind the scenes, in the green room—in the very back of your mind and the very depth of your soul—you always have a sneaking suspicion that you might not be the you that you think you are. The Germans call this a hintegedanka, a thought way back in your head that you will hardly admit to yourself, because if you were brought up in the Hebrew-Christian tradition, it would be very wicked indeed to think that you were God. That would be blasphemy; and don't you ever dare think such an idea! Of course this is all as it should be, because the show must go on until the time does come to stop.

Now you will see that these different images of the universe involve two quite different ways of dealing with two fundamental questions. The first question is, What is man? That is, Who are you? In the Hebrew-Christian answer, we more or less say, "I'm me. I am Alan Watts, John Doe, or Mary Smith, and I firmly believe that's who I am, because I really oughtn't to think anything else, ought I?" And this "me" is a finite ego, or a finite mind, whatever that is. On the other hand, the Hindu will say that atman is what we really are. We're the works, the which than which there is no whicher, the root and ground of the universe and of reality.

The next question answered differently by the two traditions is, Why have things gone wrong? Why is there evil; why is there pain; why is there tragedy? In the Christian tradition you must attribute evil to something besides God. God is defined as good, and He originally created the scheme of things without any evil in it. However, in a mysterious accident, one of the angels, called Lucifer, did not do what he was told. And there was the Fall of Man. Man disobeyed, and went against the law of God, and from that point on evil was introduced into the scheme of things and things began to go wrong, in defiance of the will of the perfectly good creator.

The Hindu thinks in a different way. He feels that the creator or the actor is the author of both good and evil because, as I explained, you have to have the evil for there to be a story. In any case, it is not as if the creator had made evil and made someone else its victim. This is not saying "God creates the evil as well as the good, and he inflicts evil upon us poor little puppets." The Hindu says, "Nobody experiences pain except the Godhead." You are not some separate little puppet who is being kicked around by omnipotence. You are omnipotence in disguise. So there is no victim of this, no helpless, defenseless, poor little thing. Even the baby with an incurable disease is the dreaming Godhead.

This viewpoint makes people brought up in the West extremely uneasy, because it seems to undercut the foundations of moral behavior. They say, "If good and evil are created by God, isn't this a universe in which anything goes? If I realize that I am God in disguise, I can get away with murder." But think it through. Didn't I point out that in the game as the Hindus analyze it, the evil part has one-third of the time and the good part has two-thirds? You will find out that all good games, games worth playing, that arouse our interest, are constructed like this. If you have the good and the evil equally balanced, the game is boring; nothing happens, it is a stalemate. The irresistible force meets the immovable object. On the other hand, if it is mostly good and there is hardly any evil, maybe just a teenie little fly in the ointment, it also gets boring. For example, suppose you knew the future, and could control it perfectly. What would you do? You would say, "Let's shuffle the deck and have another deal." When great chess players sit down to a match and it suddenly becomes apparent to both of them that white is going to mate in sixteen moves and nothing can be done about it, they abandon the game and begin another. They do not want to continue if they already know the outcome. There would not be any "hide," any element of surprise, if they knew. Again, good and evil equally balanced is not a good game, and a game with positive or good forces clearly triumphant is not an interesting game. What we want is a game where it always seems that the good side is about to lose, is in really serious danger of losing, but then always manages to sneak out a victory. In serial stories, at the end of every installment the hero is always in some absolutely impossible position—he's going to be run over by a train, and he's tied with his girlfriend to the rails. You know the author is going to get him out of his difficulty, but he mustn't do it too obviously, because that would be boring, and you wouldn't keep reading the installments. So what is necessary is a system in which the good side is always winning but is never the winner, where the evil side is always losing but is never the loser. That is a very practical arrangement for a game that will keep everybody interested.

Watch this principle at work in practical politics. Every in-group of nice people finds that it needs an out-group of nasty people so that its members will know who they are. If you are part of the in-group, you must recognize that the out-group is your necessary enemy, whom you need. Therefore you mustn't obliterate it, because if you do you are in a very dangerous state of affairs. So you have to love your enemies, and regard them as highly necessary adversaries to be respected. We need our enemies and they need us. The thing is to cool it and maintain what I call a contained conflict. When conflicts get out of hand, all sides blow up. Of course I suppose even then there will be another game, in maybe a million years.

Now, let me put these visions of the world together. If you believe the Christian, Hebrew, and Islamic view, you can't admit the Hindu view, because if you are an orthodox Christian, an orthodox Protestant Bible type, or a Roman Catholic, the one thing you cannot believe is that you are God. But let us go back to Judaism for a minute and ask the question, "If Judaism is the true religion, can Christianity also be true?" No, because the one thing in Christianity the Jew cannot admit is that Jesus Christ was God. It is unthinkable for a Jew that any man was indeed God in the flesh.

The next question, then, is, If Christianity is the true religion, can Judaism also be true? The answer is yes, because all Christians are Jews. They have accepted the Jewish religion—in the form of the Old Testament—into their own religion. Every Christian is a Jew with a particular attitude toward Jesus of Nazareth.

Let's play this game once again and ask, "If Christianity is true, can Hinduism also be true?" The answer is no, because the Christians will say, "Jesus of Nazareth was God, but you are not."

The final question is, If Hinduism is true, can Christianity be true as well? The answer is yes, because it can include Christianity. But how? What attitude would a Hindu have toward a very sincere and convinced Christian? He would say, "Bravo, absolutely marvelous; what an actor! Here in this Christian soul God is playing His most extraordinary game. He is believing and feeling that He is not Himself, and not only that, but He is living only one life, and in that life He has got to make the most momentous decision imaginable." In the course of the Christian's four score years and ten, he must choose between everlasting beatitude and everlasting horror. And he is not quite sure how to do it, because in Christianity there are two sins, among others, to be avoided. One is called presumption: knowing surely that you are saved. The other is despair: knowing surely that you are damned. There is always a margin of doubt about being damned or saved, so you work out your salvation in fear and trembling.

Thus Christianity is preeminently the gambler's religion. Imagine you know at some great casino, late at night, that there is some marvelous master gambler who has been winning, winning, winning all night. Then suddenly he decides to stake his whole winnings on whether the ball lands on red or black. Everybody gathers from all over the casino to watch this terrific gamble. In the same way, the predicament in which the Christian soul finds itself is this colossal gamble, in a universe that might possibly contain within it ultimate tragedy, an absolute, final, irremediable mistake. What a horror that thought is! So the Hindu is sitting in the audience fascinated by this Christian's extraordinary gamble. He says, "That's a beautiful game." The Christian does not know it is a game, but the Hindu suspects it is. And he is a little bit admiring of it, but not quite involved.

Perhaps you would say, "Once to every man and nation comes the moment to decide, in the strife twixt truth and falsehood, for the good or evil side. Then it is the brave man chooses while the coward stands aside." That old song sounds great, doesn't it? Commitment; stand up and be counted. This is a virtue, but on the other hand, there is another virtue, which is called being a good sport. If your enemy in the battle of life is to be regarded as an absolute enemy, pure evil as black as black can be, you cannot be a good sport and you can accord him no chivalry, no honors of battle. You have to annihilate him by any means possible, fair or foul. And that leads to some pretty sticky situations, especially when he has the means of annihilating you in just the same way.

If, on the other hand, in all contests you know that while you are going to take it seriously and regard it as very important, in the back of your mind you know it is not ultimately important. Although it is very important, you are saved, and this enables you to be a good player. You may worry about the word *play* because we often use that word in a trivial sense: "You're just playing. You mean life is nothing but a game." The Hindus indeed call the creation of the universe the *lila,* or the game, or the play of the divine. But we, too, use "play" in more profound senses. When you see *Hamlet,* which is by no means trivial, you are still seeing a play. In church the organist plays the organ. And in the Book of Proverbs, it is written that the divine wisdom created the world by playing before the throne of God. When we play music—even the music of Bach, to name a great master of what we call serious music—we are still playing.

The Hindus see this world as "play," in the deeper sense of the word, and therefore they see the intense situations, personally, socially, and so on, in which we are all involved not as bad illusions but as magnificent illusions, so well acted that they have got most of the actors fooled into forgetting who they are. When he has become fooled, man thinks of himself as a little creature that has come into this strange and foreign world, and is just a little puppet of fate. He has forgotten that the whole thing has, at its root, a playful self that is also your own self.

RELIGION AND SEXUALITY

CHAPTER SIX

I n a very special and peculiar way, Western man is hung up on sex. The major reason for this is his religious background, which is quite unique among the religions of the world. I mean specifically Christianity, and in a secondary way, Judaism, insofar as Judaism in Europe and the United States is strongly influenced by Christianity. Of all religions in the world, Christianity is the one that is most uniquely preoccupied with sex, more so than tantric yoga or any kind of fertility cult that has ever existed on the face of the earth. There has never been a religion in which sexuality was so important.

In popular speech, when you say a person is living in sin, you know very well that you do not mean that they are engaged in a business to defraud the public by the sale of badly made bread, or setting up a check forgery business. People who are living in sin are those who have an irregular sexual partnership. In the same way, when you say something is immoral, it most often means something sexually irregular. When I was a boy in school, I remember we used to have a preacher who came to us once every year, and he always talked on the subject of drink, gambling, and immorality. The way he rolled it around his tongue, it was very clear what immorality was.

Most churches in America, England, and other parts of the Western world are, frankly, sexual regulation societies, and precious little else. They occasionally get excited about other moral issues, but really not very often. To prove this you only have to ask what people can be thrown out of a church for. A person can live in envy, hatred, malice, and all uncharitableness and still be in perfectly good standing. But the moment anything about their sexual life becomes a little unusual, out they go, and that is about the only thing for which they can be removed.

For example, the Roman Catholic manuals of moral theology are technical books about sins of all kinds—what they are, how they are done, how grave they are—mostly for the advice of confessors. They are always arranged according to the Ten Commandments, and "Thou shalt not commit adultery" occupies two-thirds of the whole book, with all the details.

In a very special way, we have got sex on the brain, which is not exactly the right place for it. This needs examination, because it is not as simple as it looks. There are really two roots of the problem. One of them is the question of why, of all pleasures, religious people are particularly afraid of sexual pleasure. This is true not only of Christianity. Christianity emphasizes it in a certain way, but in Asian religions also, and especially in India, there is a prevailing view that if you want to attain real heights of spirituality, the one thing you must give up is sexuality, in the ordinary sense of genital sexual relationships. This reflects an attitude to the physical world, because it is through sexuality that we have, along with eating, our most fundamental relationship to materiality, to nature, to the physical universe. It is also the point at which we can become most attached to the body, to the physical organism and to material life. That is one reason why sexuality is problematic.

The other reason, which is more subtle, is that sexuality is something you cannot get rid of. Do what you may, life is sexual, in the sense that you are either male or female. There are various other gradations, but basically they are all forms of maleness and femaleness. And, of course, every one of you is the result of sexual intercourse. This sexual feature of life can be looked at in one of two ways. You can say, on the one hand, that all man's higher ideals, his spirituality and so forth, are simply repressed sexuality; on the other hand, you can say that human sexuality is a physical manifestation, a particular form or expression of what is spiritual, metaphysical, or divine. I hold to the latter view. I do not think that religion is repressed sexuality. Sexuality is just one of the many forms in which whatever all this is expresses itself. And sexuality is something you cannot get rid of. A way of life in which sexuality is in some way put down or repressed is nonetheless an expression of sexuality. If you realize this, then you come to a view of Christianity in which sex is a very special and unusual taboo.

And sex is taboo in Christianity; there is simply no getting around that. Up-to-date ministers today say sex is all right if you are married and you have a mature relationship with a member of the opposite sex. But if you read anything in Christian writings prior to approximately 1850, you will find that it is not all right at all. It is tolerated between married couples for the procreation of children, but on the whole it is best to do without. As Saint Paul put it, it is better to marry than to burn in hell. In all the writings of the church fathers from Saint Paul himself to Saint Ignatius Loyola to any of the great relatively modern leaders of Catholic spirituality, to Calvin and the great Protestants like John Knox, on the whole sex is sin and sex is dirt.

You can say very simply that this is very wrong, but I want to point out that there is another side to sexual prohibition. There is no way of making a hedge grow like pruning it. There is no way of making sex interesting like repressing it. Therefore, as a result of all these centuries of sexual repression and associating it with dirt, the West has developed a peculiar form of eroticism. That is an aspect of this whole problem that I do not think is really very profitable to explore, but I just want to mention in passing that the whole attitude of anti-sexuality in the Christian tradition is not as "anti" as it looks. It is simply a method of making sex prurient and exciting in a kind of dirty way. I suppose it is to be recommended to people who are not feeling very frisky and need to be pepped up.

The other side of the problem is much more interesting. That is, Why is pleasure a problem for human beings? We take sexual activity to be a supreme pleasure, and as a supreme involvement of oneself with the body and the physical world. Why should there be a problem with that? The answer is simply that the physical world is transient and impermanent; it falls apart. Bodies that were once strong, smooth, and lovely wither and become corrupt and turn at last into skeletons. If you cling to one of those bodies and it suddenly turns into a skeleton in your arms, as it will if you speed up your sense of time a little, you will feel cheated. There has been for centuries a lament about this. Life is so short, and all the beauties of this world fall apart. Therefore, if you are wise you do not set your heart on mortal beauty, you set your heart on spiritual values that are imperishable. Even Omar Khayyám says, "The worldly hope men set their hearts upon turns to ashes—or it prospers, and anon, like snow upon the desert's dusty face, lighting a little hour or two, is gone." So do not bet on that horse.

If you read any kind of spiritual literature, whether Christian, Buddhist, Hindu, or Taoist, you will find they all seem to emphasize the importance of detachment from the body, from the physical world, so that you won't be engulfed in the stream of impermanence. The idea is that, to the degree that you identify yourself with the body and with the pleasures of the body, you are simply identifying with something that will be sucked away in the course of transience. Therefore hold yourself aloof, advise many Hindus who practice yoga, and look on all sensory experiences as something out there, that you simply witness. You are to identify yourself with the eternal, spiritual, unchanging self—the witness of all that goes on—and are to be no more involved in the transitory than a mirror is involved in the things it reflects. Keep your mind pure and clean, free from dust, free from flaws, free from stain, and like a mirror just reflect everything that goes on without being attached.

It has always seemed to me that this attitude of essential detachment from the physical universe raises then the very serious question of why then have a physical

95

universe at all? If God is in some way responsible for the existence of creation, and if this creation is basically a snare, why did He do it?

According to some theologies, the physical universe is looked on as a mistake, as a fall from the divine state, as if something went wrong in the heavenly domain, causing spirits, such as we are, in fact, to fall from their highest state and become involved with animal bodies. There is an ancient analogy, which runs right through to the present time, that your relationship to your body is that of a rider to a horse. Saint Francis called his body Brother Ass. You are a rational soul in charge of an animal body, and therefore if you belong to the old school, you beat it into submission. Or if you are a Freudian you treat your horse not with a whip but kindly, with lumps of sugar; but it is still your horse. Even in Freud there is a very strong element of Puritanism. Read Phillip Rieff's book, *Freud: The Mind of the Moralist*. In it he shows that Freud basically thought that sex was something degrading, though nevertheless unavoidable and terribly necessary, which could not be swept aside but had to be dealt with. But there is still in this the heritage of thinking of ourselves as divided, of the ego as the rational soul of spiritual origin and the physical body as the animal component. Therefore, in this heritage, all spiritual success requires the spiritualization of the animal component, the sublimation of its dirty and strange urges. I suppose the ideal sexual relationship of such persons would be held on an operating table under disinfectant sprays.

Of course, it is true that the physical world and its beauty is transient. We are all falling apart in some way or other, especially after we pass the peak of youth. But this has never struck me as something to gripe about. That the physical world is transient seems to be part of its splendor. I can imagine nothing more awful than attaining the age of thirty and suddenly being frozen in that age for always. You would become a kind of animated waxworks; people with a physical permanence like that would feel like plastic. As a matter of fact, that is what is going to be done about us by technology in order to provide perpetual youth. All the parts of our bodies that decay and fold up are going to be replaced by very skillfully manufactured plastic parts, so that in the end we will be entirely made of very sophisticated plastic. Everybody will feel like plastic, and everybody will be utterly bored with each other, because the very fact that the world is always decaying and falling away is the source of its very vitality. Vitality is change. Life is death; it is always falling apart.

There are certain supreme moments when, in the body, we attain superb vitality. It is just like when an orchestra is playing and the conductor wants a certain group of violinists to come in at a certain moment, and they do. That is the whole art of life, to do it at the right time. In the same way, when it comes to love, sexuality, or, equally, all the pleasures of gastronomy, timing is of the essence. You have them for a moment, and then they are gone, but that is not something that one should look on with regret. It is regrettable only if you don't know how to accept it when its moment arrives.

This is really the essence of what I want to talk about, because to be detached from the world, in the sense that Buddhists and Taoists and Hindus often talk about detachment, does not mean to be nonparticipative. You can have a very rich and full sexual life, and yet all the time be detached. By that I do not mean that you just go through it mechanically and have your thoughts elsewhere. I mean a complete participation, but still detached. The difference between the two attitudes is this: On the one hand, there is a way of being so anxious about physical pleasure, so afraid that you won't make it, that you grab it too hard and destroy it completely. After every failed attempt to get it you feel disappointed and empty; you feel something was lost, and so you have to keep repeating, repeating, repeating. This is the hang-up. This is what is meant by attachment to this world, in the negative sense of the word. Pleasure in its fullness cannot be experienced when one is grasping it.

I knew a little girl to whom someone gave a bunny rabbit. She was so delighted with it and so afraid of losing it that taking it home in the car she squeezed it to death. Lots of parents do that to their children, and to each other. They hold on too hard, and so take the life out of this transient, beautifully fragile thing that life is. To have life and its pleasure you must, at the same time, let go of it. Then you can feel perfectly free to have that pleasure in the most gutsy, rollicking, earth-shaking, lip-licking way, with one's whole being taken over by a kind of undulative, convulsive ripple, like the very pulse of life itself. But, this can happen only if you let go, if you are willing to be abandoned.

That word, *abandoned,* is funny. We speak of people who are dissolute as being abandoned, but abandoned is also a characteristic of a saint. A great spiritual book by a Jesuit father is called *Abandonment to Divine Providence.* There are people who just are not hung up. They are those who, out of their spirituality, do not cling to any property. They do not carry burdens around. They are free, and just that sort of let-go-ness is quite essential for the enjoyment of any kind of pleasure at all, and particularly sexual pleasure.

I do not know how typical this would be of children brought up in a religious environment in the United States, but my experience as a boy in school in England was quite fascinating. When a child is baptized and is too young to know anything about its meaning, its godfather and godmother are the sponsors. When you are about to enter into puberty, however, and are confirmed, you yourself undertake your own baptismal vows. In confirmation into the Church of England, which is Episcopalian in this country, confirmation is preceded by instruction. In England this instruction consisted very largely of lessons in church history, because the British approach to religion is peculiarly archeological, based on the great Christian saints and heroes of the past. It is really quite interesting, because it somehow associates you with the tradition of King Arthur and the Knights of the Round Table, and all that sort of thing. But the time comes when every candidate for confirmation has a private talk with the school chaplain. In every process of initiation into mysteries, from time immemorial, there has been the passing on of a secret. So there is a certain anticipation about this very private communication, because you would think that, being initiated into a religion, the secret would consist of some marvelous information about the nature of God or the fundamental reason for being. But it is not so. Instead, the initiatory secret talk was a serious lecture on the evils of masturbation. What these evils were was not clearly specified, but it was vaguely hinted that ghastly diseases would result. So, in a perverse sort of way, we candidates for confirmation used to enjoy tormenting ourselves with imagining what kind of terrible diseases—venereal disease, epilepsy, tuberculosis, or the great Siberian itch—would result from this practice.

The extraordinary thing is that the very chaplain who gave these lectures had, in his own upbringing, been given the same lecture by other chaplains, and I imagine this went back some distance in history. Of course they all knew perfectly well that one of the characteristic behavior patterns of adolescence is ritual defiance of authority. You have to make some protest against authority, and in doing so you are in league with all your contemporaries, your peer group. Nobody would dream of giving anybody else away, because then he would be a tattletale, a skunk, and definitely not one of the boys. Therefore, obviously, masturbation provided the ideal outlet for this ritual defiance because it was fun, it was also an assertion of masculinity, and it was very, very wicked.

In the religious background of the Western world, we have mainly two traditions, one is Semitic, and the other is Greek. So far as the Semitic tradition is concerned, the material world and sexuality are definitely good things. Both Jews and Muslims think that God's creation of beautiful women was a grand idea. *The Perfumed Garden,* the Arabic book that is the Islamic version of the *Kama Sutra,* opens with a prayer to Allah that is a very full, detailed thanksgiving for the loveliness of women, with which Allah has blessed mankind. In the Book of Proverbs, we are enjoined to enjoy our wives while they are young. But even so, on the whole it is the Semitic belief that sexuality is justified solely for purposes of reproduction. This is what makes it good in the eyes of God, and that is the limitation put on it. Sexual energy should not really be wasted for other purposes.

In contrast to this we have a Greek tradition that was strongly influenced by a dualistic view of the universe, in which material existence is conceived of as a trap, a fall into turgid, clogging matter that is antagonistic to the lightness and freedom of the spirit. Therefore, for certain kinds of Greek religions—among which we must name the Orphic Mysteries, the Neoplatonic point of view, and the late agnostic points of view—being

saved means being delivered from material existence into a purely spiritual state. From this point of view, sexual involvement is the very archetype of material environment—*martyr, mother, mater,* and *matter,* are really the same word. So the love of woman is the great snare. This is, incidentally, a doctrine invented by men. It goes back to the words of Adam, "The woman that thou gavest me, she tempted me, and I did eat."

In the development of Christian theology, from approximately the time of Saint Paul through the beginning of the Renaissance, it was universally held that sex was a bad thing. Read Saint Augustine; he said that in the Garden of Eden before the Fall, reproduction took place in just the same place and with just the same lack of excitement as one excretes, or passes water. There was no shameful excitation of the sexual parts. The whole attitude of the church fathers in those centuries was that the virgin state was immensely superior spiritually to the marriage state, and that sexual relationships were excusable only within the bonds of marriage and for the sole purpose of reproduction. The manuals and moral penitentiaries of the theologians of the Middle Ages list all sorts of penances that must be said, even by married couples who performed sexual intercourse on the night before attending mass or receiving Holy Communion. Of course, sex must be avoided completely on certain great church festivals. Although in theory marriage is a sacrament that somehow blesses this peculiar relationship, there is a definite attitude that even within that sacrament sex is still dirty and not very nice.

You must realize, also, that in those days the institution of marriage was not what it is today. Marriage at the time of the rise of Christianity was a social institution for creating alliances between families. You did not marry the person of your choice except under the most unusual circumstances. You married the girl your family picked out for you, and they thought it over carefully from its political point of view, as well as from the point of view of eugenics, and economics. You married this girl even though you were not necessarily in love with her, and it was perfectly well understood in the secular world that on the side you had other arrangements. If you could afford them, you had concubines or even second and third and fourth wives. There was somewhat more freedom of choice about those subsidiary wives, but the first one was definitely a family arrangement. That is the context of the church's saying that only that woman whose marriage has been arranged by paternal authority should be your bedfellow.

The idea of romantic love does not arrive in connection with marriage until the troubadour cults of Provence in Southern France in the late Middle Ages. Then begins the idealization of woman as the inspiring goddess, and also the idea of the knight-errant. Dante's Beatrice is the inspiring woman who leads him to heaven. Historians today are not agreed as to whether the ladyloves of the chivalrous knights were in fact their mistresses or were simply idealized women, but the influence of the cult of romantic love on the West was profound. And it brought about a weird combination of ideas: first, the notion of the married state being the only licit relationship in which sexual play might be carried on, and second, the notion that the girl you marry should be the one with whom you have fallen in love. Two more ill-adjusted ideas could hardly be put together, because naturally when you love someone very much indeed, in your enthusiasm to become involved you say things that are hardly logical, or rational. You may stand up before an altar and say, "My darling, my sweetheart, my perfect pet, I adore you so much that I will live with you forever and ever, until death do us part." Although that is the way you feel at the time, this level of enthusiasm may not last. In a rather similar mood, ancient people would hail their kings and say, "O King, live forever." Obviously this was not meant literally; they were just wishing him a long life.

The trouble was that when that kind of extravagant poetic expression fell into the hands of people like Augustine and Totalian, who were rather influenced by Roman literalists, they wrote it into the law books. Thereby an amazing situation came about, and we still have not fully explored its subtlety. Consider certain periods when this attitude of prudery toward sexuality was in ascendancy. Nearest to our time is the bourgeois revolution in Victorian England and the United States. *Victorian* is usually a term of invective indicating extreme monogamy and a definite disgust for all things sexual. Yet, when really examining the history of the Victorian period, we find that it was an extremely lascivious epoch. One has only to look at the lushness of Victorian furniture to realize that chairs were disguised women; even the way piano legs were shaped reflects this influence.

People like Freud and Havelock Ellis made a certain mistake. They said the church, and religion in general, was nothing but a form of sublimated sex. They said, "For whatever curious reasons these people suppressed sex, and therefore it became a very powerful force for them." To understand this you must remember that they used a hydraulic analogy of human psychology. They likened it to a river—if you dammed it up, it could burst the dam. It does not actually follow that human psychology is akin to hydraulics, but this is the metaphor Ellis and Freud used. They said, "The church has repressed sex, but if you look at its symbolism you will see that it is actually a robust expression of sexuality. Everything is reduced to libido as the fundamental reality," they said. The church replied to this by saying, "It is nothing of the kind. Reducing the church to repressed sex is just a way of attacking holy things, and on the contrary, we would say that people who are fascinated with sex and make it their god are repressing religion."

The problem in this debate is that everybody has missed the boat. The church should have said to Freud, "Thank you very much. Yes indeed, our symbolism is sexual. The steeples of our churches, the vesicle-shaped windows and heraldic shields on which we put images of the crucifix or the Virgin Mother of God, these are all quite plainly sexual. However, the sexual form reveals the mysteries of the universe. Sex is not mere sex. It is a holy thing, and one of our most marvelous revelations of the divine." But the church just could not say that.

When one looks at Tibetan Buddhist iconography and images, or Hindu temples, one finds things that Europeans and Americans have never been able to understand. Here are images of buddhas and the gods engaged in amazing diversions with their female counterparts. Everybody thinks that these are dirty sculptures, but they are nothing of the kind. They reveal to the people who look at them that the play of man and woman is, on the level of biology, a reflection of the fundamental play of the cosmos. The positive and negative principles, the light and the dark, the mental and the material, all play together. The purpose of sexual play is not merely the utilitarian function of reproducing the species, as it seems to be among animals to a very large extent. What peculiarly distinguishes human sexuality is that it brings the partners closer and closer to each other in an intense state of united feeling. In other words, it is a sacrament, the outward and visible sign of an inward and spiritual grace, that brings about love. So, as that union seems to be peculiar to human beings, it is perfect nonsense to degrade human sexuality by saying it should only be carried on in the way that animals must, because they have not yet evolved to the place where sex is a sacramental expression of love. Falling in love, while considered by practical people to be a sort of madness, is actually the same sort of thing as the mystical vision, or grace. In this light we see people in their divine aspect. When the song says "Every little breeze whispers Louise," it is singing that there is a sort of extraordinary state of mystical intoxication in which every woman becomes a goddess and, likewise, every man becomes a god.

What happened, however, as a result of this conflict between the proponents of religion and the proponents of scientific naturalism was mutual name-calling. They have never come together because neither the church nor the opponents of the church has clearly understood that sexuality and all that goes with it is a triggering forth, on the level of biology, of what the whole universe is about—and that is ecstatic play. As a result, there has been a kind of compromise. In ecclesiastical circles, sex is being damned with faint praise. People are saying, "After all, sex was made by God, and perhaps it is something more than reproduction, it may bring about the cementing of the marriage ties between husband and wife," but in practice it remains the frightening taboo.

At the same time, the opposition to Christian prudery always goes overboard in the direction of total license. So we have a contest between the people who want skirt hems down to the floor and the people who want them pulled up over the head, and it seems you have to draw the line somewhere. The play between these forces is over the question of where we shall draw the line, and that is very exciting play, providing neither side wins. Imagine what it would be like if the libertines won and they took over the church on Wednesday evenings so the young Presbyterian group could meet for prayer through sex. Every child would go to the school physician for a course in hygienics, and they would have classes and plastic models, and then the children would do it in class in a very hygienic atmosphere. Imagine how boring it would all become in this setting. So the people who say that modesty is important are saying something that is quite right. They must not be allowed to prevail, but they must not be obliterated either. In life the balance of oppositions works that way.

To use an entirely different analogy, take a given biological group, a species we will call A. It has a natural enemy, B. One day A gets furious at its natural enemy B and says, "Let us obliterate B. They gather their forces and knock out their enemy. After a while, they begin to get weak and overpopulated. There is nobody around to eat up their surplus members, and they do not have to keep their muscles strong to defend against any enemy. They begin to fall apart because they have destroyed their enemy, and they remember that what they should do is cultivate the enemy. That is the real meaning of "Love your enemy." There is such a thing as a beloved enemy. If the flies and the spiders did not have each other, there would be either too many spiders or too many flies. These balances maintain the course of nature.

It is exactly the same with the libertines and the prudes. They need each other. If you have a prudish father and mother, you should be very grateful to them for having made sex so interesting. Still, every generation must react to the one before it, and this keeps the tension going. It is by this play of opposites that we know separation and seek the love that makes the world go round.

ALAN WATTS AUDIO COLLECTIONS
Original Live Recordings
from Electronic University

USING STATE-OF-THE-ART technology, Electronic University has captured and enhanced the natural sound from the original recordings so that the insights from one of this century's most notable philosophers come through as clearly as the day Alan Watts first spoke them.

The Tao of Philosophy — Volume I
ISBN 1-882435-10-9

❏ *Slices of Wisdom*—Notable segments drawn from the first thirteen weeks of the *Love of Wisdom* public radio series. (29 min.)

❏ *Images of God*—Watts explores the metaphysics underlying feminine symbolism in images of the divine throughout the world, in which "the deep" and "the dark" are recognized as the unifying ground of being. (29 min.)

❏ *Sense of Nonsense*—Recorded live on KPFA, this popular program is a delightful excursion into the essential purposelessness of life. (29 min.)

❏ *Coincidence of Opposites*—Just as the purpose of dancing is not to arrive at a certain place on the floor, life has no concrete goal to be achieved. (29 min.)

❏ *Seeing Through the Net*—In a sparkling 1969 talk to IBM systems engineers, Watts describes the "net" of perception we throw over reality, and the contrasting perceptions of "prickles" and "goo." (58 min.)

The Tao of Philosophy — Volume II
ISBN 1-882435-11-7

❏ *Myth of Myself*—What do we mean when we use the word *I*? Could self-image be the barrier to knowing who and what we really are? (42 min.)

❏ *Man and Nature*—Western culture sees the world as a mechanical system, while Eastern philosophies see it as an all-encompassing organic process. Just as an apple tree "apples," the earth "peoples," and we are not so much born into this world as grown out of it. (56 min.)

❏ *Symbols and Meaning*—As symbols, words point to things they represent, and thus have meaning. By contrast, life itself does not stand for anything else and therefore has no meaning in the usual sense. (29 min.)

❏ *Limits of Language*—Watts suggests that language may alter our view of reality, and by knowing the limits of language we can move on to the unspeakable. (29 min.)

The Philosophies of Asia — Volume I
ISBN 1-882435-12-5

❏ *Relevance of Oriental Philosophy*—Alan Watts looks at Eastern thought in contrast with the religions of the Western world. Chinese and Indian models are used to point out how we can better understand our own culture by contrasting it with others. (56 min.)

❏ *Mythology of Hinduism*—An engaging overview of the Hindu perspective on the universe, its theory of time, and the concept of an underlying godhead that is dreaming all of us. (54 min.)

❏ *EcoZen*—Speaking before a college audience, Watts points out that "ecological awareness" and "mystical experience" are different ways of saying the same thing. (29 min.)

❏ *A Ball of Hot Iron*—Continuing an introduction toward the understanding of Zen Buddhism, Watts describes the essential unity of the organism and its environment. (29 min.)

The Philosophies of Asia — Volume II
ISBN 1-882435-13-3

❏ *Intellectual Yoga*—In a lively discussion of the intellect as a path to one's enlightenment, Watts observes that "it is amazing how many things there are that aren't so." (42 min.)

❏ *Introduction to Buddhism*—Buddhism is traced from its origins in India to China, and then on to Japan. Along the way Watts brings to life one of the world's great religious traditions in its many forms, from the Theravada school to contemporary Zen. (58 min.)

❏ *Taoist Way of Karma I*—The word *karma* literally means "doing," and is thus "your doing" or action. Taoism suggests a spontaneous course of action in accord with the current and grain of nature. (29 min.)

❏ *Taoist Way of Karma II*—By following the Tao, or course of nature, one comes into harmony with the world and drops out of the cycles of karma perpetuated by our attempts to control destiny. (29 min.)

Myth and Religion — A Thorn in the Flesh

Each of these six controversial lectures challenges listeners to go beyond their usual mindsets to startling revelations about our most deep-rooted intellectual constructs. Not for the faint of heart!

❏ Not What Should Be, Not What Might Be, But What Is! (58 mins.)

❏ Spiritual Authority (58 mins.)

❏ Jesus: His Religion, or the Religion About Him? (58 mins.)

❏ Democracy in the Kingdom of Heaven (58 mins.)

❏ Image of Man (58 mins.)

❏ Religion and Sexuality (58 mins.)

Buddhism —The Religion of No-Religion

In a variety of settings from Kyoto to Sausalito, Alan Watts joyfully takes us on a journey to Buddhism, from its roots in India to the explosion of interest in Zen and the Tibetan tradition in the West. While on tour in Japan with a small group in 1965, Watts spoke daily, offering a step-by-step explanation of the development of the major schools, terms, and perspectives of Buddhism. Talks from the Japan seminars are complemented by two sessions recorded in 1969 aboard Watts's ferryboat home near San Francisco.

❑ The Journey from India I (29 mins.)

❑ The Journey from India II (29 mins.)

❑ Buddhism as Dialogue (58 mins.)

❑ Following the Middle Way (58 mins.)

❑ Religion of No-Religion (58 mins.)

❑ Wisdom of the Mountains (58 mins.)

❑ Transcending Duality (29 mins.)

❑ Diamond Web (29 mins.)

New Series

❑ **Eastern and Western Zen**—Zen Stories (50 min); Uncarved Block, Unbleached Silk (44 min.); Biting the Iron Bull (45 min.); Swimming Headless (51 min.); Wisdom on the Ridiculous (46 min.); Zen Bones (59 min.)

❑ **Philosophy and Society**—On Time and Death (50 min.); The Cosmic Drama (45 min.); Philosophy of Nature (45 min.); What Is Reality? (50 min.); Mysticism and Morals (58 min.); On Being God (60 min.)